A Culinary History of
WEST
VIRGINIA

A Culinary History of
WEST
VIRGINIA

FROM RAMPS TO
PEPPERONI ROLLS

•SHANNON COLAIANNI TINNELL•

AMERICAN PALATE

The West Virginia skies are blue,
The hills are green and hearts are true;
A joyous welcome waiteth you,
In West Virginia.

—Howard Llewellyn Swisher, "In West Virginia"

Published by American Palate
A Division of The History Press
Charleston, SC
www.historypress.com

First published 2020

Manufactured in the United States

ISBN 9781625859259

Library of Congress Control Number: 2019956038

For my family

History is who we are and why we are the way we are.
—David McCullough

CONTENTS

INTRODUCTION

I t is impossible to document the history of a place, or even a specific aspect of that place's history, without taking into account its cultural geography. Cultural geography examines how and where humans choose to live, build homes and use the land because those things contribute fundamentally to everyday lives and traditions, influencing how a culture dresses, the art they make and what customs they may practice and why. Cultural geography also explores what and how a culture eats.

West Virginia's culture and identity were, and are, greatly shaped by the land itself and the weather and soil and terrain that dictated what could be grown or otherwise harvested and when. Foods were tied to location and season, and the resultant connection created traditions that stubbornly persist among the peoples of the Mountain State. The history of West Virginia cannot be told without telling the story of its inhabitants' relationship with their foods and foodways.

Foodways are the social, economic and cultural practices related to the production and consumption of food. It is the study of what we eat, how we eat, how we prepare food, how we preserve food, where we get food, who we get it from, when we eat and what we do with it. Our attitudes, practices and rituals around food define who we are and what we believe.

This book is a study of West Virginia foodways and specifically how those foodways shape the regional identity of the state. West Virginia's foodways are a microcosm of the larger story of American food and foodways, particularly Appalachian culinary customs and traditions. West Virginia is composed of a mixture of people with their own cultural identities and customs, all of which have shaped the state's identity. The first people to live in the area were the indigenous tribes of Native Americans, followed by waves of successive settlers from early European explorers through colonial-era pioneers to African Americans and European immigrants drawn by the Industrial Revolution's promise of a better life in the New World. The foodways of West Virginia reflect not only all of these different cultures but also a subsequent fusion of their various characteristics into West Virginia culture, as well as the integration of local foods into their foodways.

Given that we all must eat to stay alive, it stands to reason that we all are connected to food, although it is also a given that many of us have allowed that connection to become stretched, strained and forgotten. In the past, prior to the effects of mass production and industrial farming, the connection to food was more direct, more conscious—even among people who dwelt in urban areas. Then and now, regardless of how conscious we are of this connection, it still very much exists, defined by a number of conditions, whether naturally occurring—think geography, climate, soil type and the presence or absence of natural resources—or examples grounded in technology and human intervention, such as industrial refrigeration and cheap, long-distance transportation of goods. Without question, cultures developed around the pursuit of food, most famously exemplified by the movement away from the hunter/gatherer culture to organized agriculture, which in turn led to permanent settlements, which in turn led to the development of concentrated populations and the birth of urban living. But the rise of agriculture led to more than the rise of cities. It also promoted social and behavioral changes. Religious ceremonies and rituals came into being and evolved, often reflecting anxiety and hope about the harvesting of crops. For some cultures, this included ritualizing the experience of eating by adopting rules for the preparation and consumption of food. As mankind spread across the globe and diversified into myriad cultures, so did food and foodways. In the modern era, technology has allowed the cultural barriers that evolved over centuries to erode, allowing—in First World countries, at least—access to a great variety of international, nonnative foods and food preparation methods, whether at a McDonald's in Berlin or a sushi bar in Iowa.

At the same time, we are witnessing a push-back against the industrialization and corporate appropriation of food, perhaps most notably in the farm-to-table or locavore movement. By demonstrating a genuine interest in where their food comes from, and by pursuing fresh and locally grown food, people are strengthening their connection to what they eat and why. Many are drawn to exploring the traditions, preparation techniques and history associated with what they are eating. This may be due to an interest in personal health, or in response to distrust of industrial farming, or even for the simple love of eating good food and wanting to extend the experience. On an even more personal level, we may find ourselves with our own unique personal and sentimental memories of food, which in turn may fuel a desire to learn more about it or to re-create earlier experiences. Because food not only satisfies our hunger and fuels our very existence but can also be a source of entertainment, of family bonding, of reconnecting with the past and connecting with our neighbors. In short, food can be fun, too. Essential, developmental, cultural, political, technological, psychological, political, entertaining—all of these words can be used to describe food and foodways around the world, and they can most certainly be used to describe food and its evolution and impact on the state of West Virginia and the people and cultures who have called it home.

Chapter 1
EARLY HISTORY

There's a surefire way to annoy a West Virginian, if indeed that is an ambition that appeals to you, and it's very simple to achieve. All you need do upon being introduced to someone and learning they are from the Mountain State is say something like, "Oh, I've been to Richmond" or "I've always wanted to go to Colonial Williamsburg." At which point, the person will politely (or perhaps not so politely) remind you that West Virginia is not Virginia. In fact, even when it was part of Virginia, it was in many ways distinctly separated from the mother state, and not just by geography, although the imposing barrier of mountains that separate the two for a great portion of their borders absolutely was an overwhelming reason those distinctions evolved. Difficulty transporting goods, a lack of soil and terrain conducive to tobacco-raising and the movement of large-scale slaveholding operations to the Deep South all contributed to a relatively small population of slave owners and the attendant lifestyle. That distance from the slaveholding culture coupled with a proximity to northern and midwestern states (and their prevailing sensibilities) were certainly strong factors in West Virginia, after breaking away from the mother state, becoming the thirty-fifth state admitted to the Union (and the only one born amid the Civil War) on June 20, 1863. As important as that date is in West Virginia's history, obviously that history does not begin on the day of its admittance to the Union any more than it began when it was first glimpsed by European explorers during the colonial era, and that includes the history of its foods and foodways. Those histories, both traditional and culinary, begin with the land itself and associated factors dating back over one billion years. Perhaps chief among those factors are the state's borders—because the borders will define the conditions that gave rise to a culture and its foodways.

West Virginia is the most northern of the southern states and the most southern of the northern states, the most eastern of the western states and the most western of the eastern states. In terms of size, West Virginia contains a little over twenty-four thousand square miles and is forty-first out of fifty states in size. West Virginia is a land of contrasts, and the landscape is no exception, with a topography that rises from 260 feet above sea level at Harpers Ferry in Jefferson County to almost 5,000 feet at Spruce Knob in Pendleton County. The state's irregular boundaries follow the natural borders of mountains, rivers and streams (along with some "man-made" contributions including the Mason-Dixon line), which give it its unusual, readily identifiable shape, thanks to not one but two protruding "panhandles." With an average elevation of 1,500 feet, it contains some of the most rugged and remote land in the United States. West Virginia has long been nicknamed "Little Switzerland" and, more popularly, the "Mountain State."

As it is the only state that lies completely within the Appalachian region, West Virginia is often called "the heart" of Appalachia. The defining characteristic of Appalachia is the presence of the Appalachian Mountains. Named after the Apalachee Indian tribe of Florida, the Appalachians are at least three hundred to five hundred million years old and are the oldest mountains in North America, and among the oldest in the world. Stretching from southern New York to northern Mississippi, the Appalachians are particularly formidable in West Virginia, creating a natural, rugged barrier and boasting incredible biodiversity, two factors that would loom large in the state's cultural and culinary evolution.

The mountains, along with rock formations, waterways and soil, are the result of a great deal of tectonic shifting, continental drift, wind, weather, erosion, flooding and other factors that presented themselves over the last billion years or so. Seas repeatedly flooded and then receded from the region. The shifting of tectonic plates gave rise to the Appalachian Mountain range. Mineralogical deposits such as coal appeared among the upheaval. The glaciers of the ice ages never reached West Virginia but had an effect nonetheless when an enormous ice dam formed in the north, creating a lake that left deposits in the northern part of the state and drainage changes and alluvial deposits (materials such as silt, sand, gravel, clay and organic matter that is deposited by streams and rivers) in the southern part. We could absolutely explore all of that history in greater detail, tripping over scientific

A 1754 map of the western land of Virginia, which would become West Virginia. *Library of Congress.*

terminology like Paleozoic Era (which was 600 to 230 million years ago), Taconic Orogeny (a mountain-building period that ended over 400 million years ago) and clastics (rocks broken down from older rocks). But thankfully, this book is dedicated to West Virginia's culinary history, and as such, we'll move on from prehistoric geological events.

With over forty mountain peaks over four thousand feet, West Virginia's identity is tied to its mountainous terrain, and with good reason. Rivers also have played a huge role in the state's natural and cultural evolution. The Ohio River has played a major role in westward expansion and, along with the Big Sandy and Tug Fork Rivers, forms the state's western border. Eventually emptying into the Mississippi River and, ultimately, the Gulf of Mexico, the Ohio is formed in Pittsburgh, Pennsylvania, by the confluence of the Allegheny and Monongahela Rivers. The dominant watershed of north-central West Virginia, the north-flowing Monongahela was one of the earliest trade and settlement routes into West Virginia and kept the northern region connected to Pennsylvanian culture, attitudes and foodways. However, the Monongahela did not allow reliable transportation into the interior, and even the eventual construction of locks and dams did not allow the sort of commercial development enjoyed by regions settled along major waterways.

In the south, the New River, which is considered the second-oldest river in the world, merges with the Gauley to form the Kanawha River. The state capital of Charleston sits along the Kanawha, as did the state's once-flourishing chemical industry, benefiting from the river being navigable to the Ohio and the opportunities it presented for commercial river traffic. In the southwestern part of the state, the Guyandotte River and Big Sandy meet with the Tug Fork to form the remaining tributaries to the Ohio within the state's boundaries, although they were not large enough for large-scale navigational opportunities.

Across the state (and the Eastern Continental Divide) flow the tributaries that give rise to the Potomac River. Beginning as a mere trickle at the Fairfax Stone on the West Virginia–Maryland border, the Potomac flows eastward, ever-expanding, merging not only with its South Branch but also a number of other smaller watersheds throughout the Potomac Highlands, as well as rivers and streams dropping out of Maryland and Pennsylvania to the north and, at Harpers Ferry, the Shenandoah River from the south. The Potomac played a huge role not only in the development and settlement of West Virginia but in American history in general. Some sixty miles downriver from Harpers Ferry, the Potomac flows through Washington, D.C., on its journey to the Chesapeake Bay and beyond to the waters of the Atlantic Ocean.

These mountains and rivers have greatly contributed to the shaping of West Virginia's four distinctive geographic regions. A geographic region can be defined as an area that shares many common features, which may in turn impact the development and preservation of culture, including foodways. West Virginia is divided into four geographic regions:

Potomac: This section was first settled by Europeans. It has gently rolling farmland and is famous for its apple and peach orchards. It is rural; close to Washington, D.C.; borders Maryland and Virginia; and, as its name suggests, is centered on the Potomac River watershed. Unlike the rest of the state, this region was, and is, relatively accessible to established Tidewater and Piedmont populations in Virginia as well as Maryland. Thus, it presents more of a colonial identity. The region is home to Berkeley Springs, a colonial-era spa, and historic Harpers Ferry, where abolitionist John Brown famously tried to arm African American slaves and start a revolution—and in the process helped jump start the Civil War. Rich in limestone, the region supports agriculture, poultry and livestock.

Allegheny Highland: This sparsely populated area is located west of the Potomac River and is home to the many peaks from which West Virginia's

Circa 1910–20 image of Sandstone Falls on the New River located in Summer County. *Detroit Publishing Company Photograph Collection, Library of Congress.*

Harper's Ferry by Moonlight. An 1874 steel engraving by R. Hinshelwood after a painting by Granville Perkins. *Library of Congress.*

nickname of the "Mountain State" was derived. The region offers beautiful outdoor scenery and vast tracts of wilderness and is popular with skiers. Settled in the late 1800s and early 1900s, the region is home to the upper reaches of the Potomac, Monongahela and Greenbrier watersheds. At one time, the timber industry and the railroads that serviced it were central to the region's identity. In fact, tourists can still experience something of that near-vanished era in the state's history courtesy of the Cass Scenic Railroad. Spruce Knob, the highest point in the state, is located here, as is the unique village of Helvetia, founded in the nineteenth century by Swiss immigrants, whose culture and foodways linger yet.

Ohio Valley: This area begins at the tip of the northern panhandle and extends southwest the full length of the state. The area includes all counties whose average altitude is less than one thousand feet above sea level and whose streams and rivers empty into the Ohio River Basin. Oil, natural gas, glass, steel and textiles were all at one time dominant industries that greatly shaped the identity of the region. The cities of Parkersburg, Wheeling and Huntington are all located within the valley.

Allegheny Plateau: The plateau area has high hills but not high enough to be mountains (1,000 to 3,500 feet) and is an elevated tract of more or less level land. The area passes through the central part of the state from south to north. The New River Gorge Bridge, on the second-oldest river in the world, is located here, as is Summersville Lake, the largest man-made lake in West Virginia and reportedly possessing water so clear that divers come to experience what is known as the "Little Bahamas." The state capital of Charleston is the largest of the region's cities. The area is rich in coal, oil, natural gas, shale, limestone and sandstone.

The very distinct differences between the regions have led to many distinctions in the cultures that have developed in each of them, and even within them. The rugged mountain ranges stymied the development of highways and railroads, and as mentioned previously, interior river traffic was very difficult to achieve. While not all the regions were isolated, they were often isolated from one another.

This isolation sometimes even occurred within a single region and not just in the mountains. In particular, consider the many differences between northern and southern West Virginia. The northern part of the state is more densely populated. In fact, the state's northern panhandle extends farther north than nearby Pittsburgh, Pennsylvania. The development of not only coal mines but also steel mills and related industries along the Ohio River drew in immigrant labor and, as such, fostered diverse communities populated by a variety of people of eastern and southern European and African American descent. The city of Morgantown is home to West Virginia University and several other large employers that have attracted a diverse population, which in turn has led to a cosmopolitan atmosphere in a town that was once a remote, colonial outpost along the Monongahela.

The farther south one travels, the more rural and less densely populated the state becomes. While there were coal mines—and often large populations accompanying them—the rise of mechanized coal extraction and periodic declines in the market resulted in a large exodus of the region's residents. The remoteness of many towns in the southern mountains, encumbered by a lack of infrastructure, stifled the development of industries and institutions that could withstand the ups and downs of the coal business. This region, particularly the large area south and southwest of Charleston, was home to the legendary Hatfield and McCoy feud and is often depicted as being representative of West Virginia as a whole, when in fact, as we have and will continue to see, the state is far more nuanced and diverse than pervasive stereotypes would have strangers believe. In fact, even within this region, these stereotypes woefully reduce what was—and is—a vibrant and diverse culture.

Helvetia's original Swiss and German settlers arrived in 1869. The remote location has helped preserve the traditions of dance, music and food. *Carol Highsmith Collection, Library of Congress.*

For over a century, West Virginia's identity has been tied to its extractive industries—namely, coal mining, but also timber, gas and even salt. But initially it was a predominantly rural region built on agriculture, and a strong connection to agriculture has survived. In fact, the West Virginia state seal features a miner alongside a farmer, clearly underlining two vocations that were chosen to represent citizens of the Mountain State. And of course, the state motto "Montani Semper Liberi," which translates to "Mountaineers Are Free," adds a third aspect to West Virginia's official "identity"—the men and women of the mountains, tied to the earliest settlers who valued freedom and pursued self-reliance. In reality, West Virginians are much more diverse in their identities, occupations and interests, although they do tend to share that one annoyance mentioned earlier: people who think West Virginia is still part of Virginia. You've been warned!

The influences of location and landscape on cultures and their foodways are pervasive. While far less extreme and clear-cut, the foodways that have evolved in West Virginia have also been shaped and modified not only by landscape, weather and geography but also by other factors, including migration and settlement, the disruptive ramifications of invasion and conquest, the rise of the Industrial Revolution and the development of transportation infrastructure. While the basic conditions affecting foodways are natural and the result of billions of years of geological and other natural events, obviously it is only with the coming of humans that the foodways of a culture can be established and evolve. In West Virginia, the human contribution to the state's culture and foodways began thousands and thousands of years ago.

Chapter 2
NATIVE AMERICANS

The first evidence of humans in West Virginia dates back to the appearance of nomadic Paleo-Indians around 11000 BCE. These individuals had no written history, and the only way we can get a glimpse into the way they lived is by examining the artifacts they left behind. The Paleo-Indians were descendants of the early hunter-gatherers who followed large animals from what is now far eastern Russia on a long-vanished land bridge crossing the Bering Strait into North America. For thousands of years after, they and their descendants settled throughout the Americas. All the Native American tribes of North America, as well as the Aztec, Mayan, Incan and other cultures in Central and South America, would develop from them. Prior to the emergence of those civilizations, however, those explorers, hunters and settlers lived during a time referred to as prehistory, the period of human activity that occurred between the use of the first stone tools, some 3.3 million years ago, and the invention of writing systems, the earliest of which appeared 5,300 years ago. Despite having no written language or records, they did leave behind artifacts, the study of which allows us to gain a better understanding of how they lived, including how and what they ate.

In West Virginia, these early people primarily lived in the Kanawha and Ohio Valleys. They hunted large mammals with fluted-stone spear points and set up butchering campsites to process these large animals. At first, they foraged what they could out of the forest, but they later learned to cultivate squash, gourds and pumpkins. The Paleo-Indians belonged to the cultural period labeled, logically, the Paleo-Indian Period. Cultural periods are used by historians, anthropologists and archaeologists to categorize civilizations and the various eras within which they existed. Culture periods are defined by several factors, including a culture's possession of similar features or conditions, environmental factors, access to resources, social structures and cultural traditions. Historians have identified four prehistory cultural periods in the Native American history of West Virginia. The Paleo-Indian Period was the first cultural period to exist in what is now the Mountain State.

The second, the Archaic Period, occurred between 8000 BC and 1000 BC. As mastodons and other large animals disappeared, it became necessary to hunt and eat smaller game. This necessity motivated the inhabitants to begin developing techniques and modifying weapons to facilitate the hunting and processing of the smaller game that was now a crucial part of their diet. They continued to forage for indigenous nuts and berries to supplement their diets. These developments mark the beginning of the Archaic Period. The period started coming to an end around four thousand years ago with the development of the production of pottery and, perhaps even more importantly, the introduction of agrarian practices. Specifically, Native Americans during this time began to cultivate corn, modifying it from its roots as a wild highland grass.

Corn was to become an important staple for the Native American peoples of the third, or Woodland, period, not least because the nature of its hulls meant the crop could be stored long term, as well as the fact that corn could be transformed into a variety of dishes. The name corn means "our life," and giving life is exactly what it did, not just for Native Americans but also for the explorers, traders and settlers to follow. The Woodland Period occurred between around 1000 BC and AD 1. Burial mounds found throughout West Virginia, especially in the Ohio and Kanawha River Valley, provide numerous examples of material culture that in turn allow a better glimpse into how these peoples lived. Material culture refers to the physical objects created by humans. It can be anything created for survival, to represent identity or to benefit an individual's mind, social or economic standing. Non-material culture is defined as the intangible components of our way of life, including language, norms, beliefs, religion, family patterns, political and economic systems.

The Grave Creek Mound is the second-largest conical earthen mound in North America and is located, logically, in the town of Moundsville, near the Ohio River. The mound currently is 62 feet high and 240 feet in diameter at the base. The Grave Creek Mound is a major West Virginia landmark. It was built by an early Woodland tribe known as the Adena, who flourished between 500 BC and AD 200. Time and again, around the world, the establishment of a farming culture has led to the development of fixed settlements and emerging civilizations, and being farmers, the Adena were no exception. Native American women invented farming, and it remained a female responsibility among the tribe. The women also foraged for wild edibles. Their agrarian practices featured sunflowers and expanded to include beans and squash along with corn. These were the forerunners of what would become known as the "three sisters"—critically important crops to Native Americans in the centuries to come. The men hunted and fished.

Manufacturing skills were evolving during the Woodland Period, and archaeology has unearthed examples of flint knives, hoes, bracelets, clay pottery and pottery tempered with crushed rock and limestone, as well as drills, arrowheads, spears and bone beads. The stability of crops that led to permanent settlement allowed the Native Americans to develop more of a culture than previous prehistoric peoples who were constantly on the move in search of large game.

The Grave Creek Mound is one of over four hundred prehistoric mounds found throughout the state. Most of these are located along the major river systems and valleys in the state, especially the Kanawha, Ohio and Potomac. Native Americans settled along these waterways, using them for transportation and economic opportunities, a pattern we would see repeated by settlers and inhabitants in the centuries to come.

The final prehistory period is the Late Prehistoric Period, which occurred between AD 100 and 1700. This period would see the development of the Native American cultures or tribes most familiar to the modern reader. The tribes closely associated with West Virginia history include the Cherokee, Delaware, Iroquois, Manahoac, Meherrin, Mingo, Monacan, Nottaway, Occaneechi, Saponi and Shawnee. Native Americans were not a cohesive unit. They had hundreds of different cultures and customs. The hunter-gatherer tradition stubbornly persisted and remained central to the foodways of the tribes, but diversification of foodways was an absolute reality. Tribal economies were based not only on hunting, trapping and fishing but also on foraging and, as discussed earlier, farming. As was to be expected, non-material culture developed with ritualistic and religious ceremonies, and practices arose in direct relation to food and foodways. For instance, Native Americans held festivals in honor of the harvest, complete with ceremonies expressing gratitude for bountiful crops and game.

FIG. 56.—GREAT MOUND AT GRAVE CREEK

The cone-shaped Grave Creek Mound located in Marshall County was constructed by the Adena culture, also known as "Mound Builders," who lived in what is now West Virginia during the Early Woodland Period (circa 1000 BC). *1848 engraving by J.W. Orr, Library of Congress.*

Material culture also evolved and expanded in pragmatic response to the needs of those doing the hunting, farming, harvesting and preparation of foods. The division of labor practiced by earlier cultures persisted. Men made weapons and tools, hunted and fished. Women took care of the homes and agricultural duties such as tending the gardens, grinding corn, dressing and curing meat and tanning hides. Native Americans cooked by boiling, broiling, drying or roasting.

Native American villages were located by good water sources. This also provided them with protection from the elements and gave them access to wood for fuel and food to hunt and forage. They also looked for land to have gardens. The agricultural practices of Native Americans in western Virginia included slash burning and the planting of the aforementioned three sisters or trinity: corn, beans and squash. Observation and trial and error through the centuries came to bear on this early, effective example of what is now known as "companion planting." Iroquois legend believed corn, beans and squash to be three inseparable sisters who can only grow and thrive together. This tradition of interplanting corn, beans and squash in the same mounds, widespread among Native American farming societies, is a sophisticated, sustainable system that contributes to long-term soil fertility. In the "three sisters" method, corn provides a natural pole for bean vines to climb. Beans fix nitrogen on their roots, improving the overall fertility of the plot by providing nitrogen to the following year's corn. Bean vines also help stabilize the corn plants, making them less vulnerable to blowing over in the wind. Shallow-rooted squash vines become a living mulch, shading emerging weeds and preventing soil moisture from evaporating, thereby improving the overall crops' chances of survival in dry years. Spiny squash plants also help discourage predators from approaching the corn and beans. The large amount of crop residue from this planting combination can be incorporated back into the soil at the end of the season to build up organic matter and improve its structure. The effectiveness of the three sisters approach continues to be celebrated today, as many modern gardeners attempt to grow produce in a more environmentally friendly, space-saving manner.

In addition to the symbiotic relationship the plants enjoy, the three sisters of squash, beans and corn also complement one another nutritionally and contribute variety to the human diet. Corn provides carbohydrates, while the dried beans are rich in protein, balancing the lack of necessary amino acids found in corn. Finally, squash yields both vitamins from the fruit and healthful, delicious oil from the seeds. Clearly, all three of the "sisters" contributed meaningfully to the Native American diet—but it was corn that was valued most of all. Corn was eaten at almost every meal. It was easy to dry for preservation and storage during the cold winter months. Dried corn was made into hominy, also called masa, using a Native American technology known as nixtamalization. This was achieved by soaking corn in an alkali solution of either lime water or wood ash in water until the kernels split open. In the area that would become West Virginia, wood ash was used. These would be drained and fried over a fire. The corrosive nature of the solution removes the hull and germ of the corn and causes the grain itself to puff up to about twice its normal size.

The hominy block is a prime example of adaptive technology employed by Native Americans to process corn. It was a primitive method used to grind corn and grains. To make a hominy block, a tree stump was hollowed out by burning. The corn was placed in the cavity of the tree before it had a chance to harden and was ground into meal using a pestle. This system obviously had its limitations and was time consuming.

Native Americans often located their villages near large rocks where mortars could be made for grinding corn. These mortars varied in size from a half bushel to a quart. Corn was placed into the hollowed-out mortar and then pounded with the pestle, which would grind it into a powdery form. After this process it became cornmeal, which could be used for cornbread, corn cakes, corn syrup, corn pudding and a thickening agent for their stews.

Later, Native Americans often intervened to ensure the survival of the white European settlers (who ultimately displaced them and all but eradicated their cultures, as we shall see in the next chapter). The "johnnycake," one of the most popular and influential dishes among the colonists, in fact originated with the native inhabitants of North America. The Algonquians of the Atlantic seaboard are credited with teaching Europeans how to make what would become a life-sustaining staple in the lives of European transplants. Johnnycakes are a cornmeal flatbread similar to pancakes and are known by many different names, including ashcake, battercake, corn cake, cornpone, hoecake, journey cake, mush bread, pone, Shawnee cake, jonakin and jonikin. The origin of these delicious and versatile cakes is something of a mystery and probably has nothing to do with the name John. They were also called journey cakes because they could be carried on long trips in saddlebags and baked along the way. Some historians think that they were originally called Shawnee cakes and that the colonists slurred the words, pronouncing it as johnnycakes. According to *What's Cooking America*, the word "johnnycake" comes from the word *janiken*, an American Indian word that means corn cake. The Native Americans ate them like crackers, crumbling them on top of their soups and stews.

Throughout North and South America, the Native Americans shared their knowledge of the harvesting and gathering of life-sustaining foods like white and sweet potatoes, tomatoes, squash and peanuts, along with a crop that was quite the opposite: tobacco.

Game was plentiful in the East, and eastern Native Americans' lifestyle reflected that reality, in contrast to, for example, the nomadic life of the Native Americans of the Great Plains, whose dependence on buffalo forced them to follow the latter's migratory patterns. The eastern Native Americans consumed a variety of meats, including bear, deer, raccoon, squirrel and rabbit. Birds were eaten and their eggs used when possible, and fishing remained a source of high-protein food.

Foraging continued to supplement the tribal diet, as it would that of the settlers who followed down to the present day. Nuts were an important, naturally occurring food source, whether eaten raw out of the shell, roasted or boiled down into a milk-like liquid. The latter was important because the Native Americans only had wolf-like dogs as domestic animals. There were no cows, sheep or goats and thus no milk source other than that provided to infants by their nursing mothers. Nut trees and shrubs native to West Virginia include hickory, black walnut, beechnuts, oaks, chinquapins and hazelnuts.

Sadly, the most important nut to the region has all but disappeared, and with it the entire ecosystem has experienced a profound disturbance. The American chestnut (*Castanea dentata*), a member of the beech family, was a rapid-growing tree that averaged about ninety feet in height. The dominant hardwood species in West Virginia and the eastern United States, in some regions the chestnut accounted for as many as one out of every four trees. The trees were so thick that when in bloom in the spring, they could give the illusion of mountains being blanketed with snow. The tree was important to Native Americans because it produced large crops of nuts that could be eaten by both wildlife and humans, unlike acorns. And in contrast to oaks, hickories and other trees that don't necessarily produce nuts every year, the chestnut reliably produced mast every year, ensuring a food source. The mast of the forest floor provided food not only for the wild game but also the Native Americans and Europeans who followed. There are those who say the taste of wild game, like turkey, has changed in the absence of the once omnipresent chestnut. The species came to be used in many ways by early European settlers, providing food and timber, food for domesticated animals and tannin.

Beginning in the early twentieth century, an exotic fungal disease, commonly known as chestnut blight, attacked chestnut trees and started to kill them at a rate of twenty-four miles per year. By the 1950s, virtually all mature American chestnuts had succumbed to the disease. Fortunately, there are ongoing efforts achieving success in bringing back a blight-resistant form of the American chestnut and restoring it to its rightful place in the Appalachian ecosystem.

The black walnut (*Juglans nigra*) is a wide-branching tree that can reach between seventy and one hundred feet in height. With twelve- to eighteen-inch compound leaves composed of seven to seventeen leaflets, the black walnut leads the transition to autumn colors. Its leaves change from green to yellow early, usually in September, and fall early as well. When crushed, they have a spicy scent. Large, round edible nuts are the "fruit" of the black walnut tree and are related to apples, cherries and plums, as they also start out as flowers. They differ by having a hard hull and only one seed. The minimum seed-bearing age for the black walnut is twelve years, and it can be an excellent source of edible nuts for both humans and wildlife. Every October, the town of Spencer hosts the West Virginia Black Walnut Festival.

A black walnut baking contest and a pancake breakfast are just two ways this nut is celebrated each year.

The black walnut tree is also one of the state's most valuable forest trees. Black walnut wood is free from warping, able to take high polish and very durable. Lumber from the black walnut tree is used for furniture, cabinets, gunstocks and veneer. In the wild, black walnut trees can be one of the scarcest of the native hardwood trees. Currently, the largest black walnut tree in the state is located at Alderson in Greenbrier County. It stands more than ninety-four feet high and has a crown spread of one hundred feet.

The black walnut tree was once a staple in everyone's backyard orchard, planted along with apple and peach trees. The nuts from this tree have a stronger taste than their English walnut cousin and are more difficult to harvest. Years ago, black walnuts would be spread out on top of farm sheds to hasten their ripening. When the nuts have turned completely black, they are easier to shuck. But be careful! As the nuts ripen, they are filled with a dark black fluid that will stain everything. The liquid was once used as ink and is still used as a natural dye.

The best time to go nut hunting is in October and November. By this time, the nuts have finished their development and are ready to drop. If you take a hike after a big storm, you'll find a carpet of nuts on a forest floor. The historical significance of the walnut in West Virginia culture is evident in the presence of place names. For example, there is a Walnut, West Virginia, in Pocahontas County; Walnut Hill in Logan County; Walnut Grove Cemeteries in Bluefield; and Walnut Ridge in Braxton County. Walnut Grove, also known as the Andrew Beirne House, is a historic home located near Union in Monroe County.

Nut trees and bushes represent but a fraction of the plants foraged by the tribes, who were adept at locating wild roots and tubers—like the sweet potato, a member of the morning glory family—and incorporating them into their diets. Seasonal impacts on the availability of different wild foods and medicines were incorporated into tribal practices, customs and foodways, as evidenced by the spring harvesting of the ramp (*Allium trioccum*), a wild leek much celebrated in West Virginia to this day.

The genus Allium also includes domestic onions, leeks, garlic, shallots, chives and an array of wild onions. Forming large clumps of tightly packed bulbs, ramps grow best in areas that have heavy snow and colder temperatures. They are often found growing on north-facing slopes and in cool ravines, usually with a stream close by. They grow along hardwood trees such as sugar maples, beech, basswood, yellow birch and elm and among native plants such as spring beauty, toothwort, Dutchman's Daughter, squirrel corn and trout lily.

Rich in minerals and vitamins A and C, these relatives of the leek family start emerging from the forest floor in late March and early April. They are one of the first greens to appear after long winters in West Virginia. They are best harvested in April and May and are ready to harvest before the forest canopy is fully formed. The smooth leaves die back and make them undetectable until the flowers bloom through June and July. By the time the flowers appear, the bulbs are too strong. The seeds from the flowers take over a year to germinate and between three and five years to produce a large bulb. They reproduce through rhizomes, root-like stems that run underground.

Ramps were highly revered by the Native Americans not only for their nutritional value but also for their medicinal properties. They used them as a tonic to treat intestinal worms, treat colds, induce vomiting and treat and prevent insect wounds. They have been used for generations throughout the state as a spring tonic and a blood purifier. Ramps also have cancer-fighting benefits, and some people claim to feel a sense of calm after eating a mess of ramps. During early settlement in the area, settlers relied on them after a long winter of having mainly meat, salt pork and dried vegetables.

Shakespeare mentioned ramps in *Henry V*, and the Grimm fairy tale "Rapunzel" is named after the plant, using the German name. In the story, a prince agrees to give his unborn child to the witch whose garden he has been taking ramps from to satisfy his wife's craving for the plant.

In medieval times, before the potato was accessible to Europe, ramp roots were cooked down and used as a starchy food source, as well as eaten fresh. The entire plant is edible.

Ramps are one of dozens of different potherbs that grow throughout the state. Potherbs are plants whose leaves, flowers or stems can be cooked and eaten. Potherbs native to West Virginia include spring beauties, nettles, giant chickweed, pokeweed, milkweed, dandelion, cress, purslane, chicory, fireweed, lamb's quarters, pansy and watercress, to name a few.

Although poke (*Phytolacca americana*) is probably the most popular and most utilized potherb in West Virginia, all parts of the plant are poisonous if eaten raw. The young spring leaves of the plant are edible, but as the plant matures, they become poisonous. Plants over nine inches tall and showing any amount of red on the plant must be avoided. For this reason, unless you really know what you are doing, it is better to collect dandelion leaves, as they are not only edible but also plentiful, as they grow everywhere, and incredibly nutritious.

Dandelion (*Taraxacum officinale*), also known as "lion's tooth," is part of the sunflower family. This family includes more than twenty-two thousand species, including daisies and thistles. The plant is rich in vitamins A and C, iron, calcium and detoxifiers. The young leaves have a milder flavor. Try adding dandelion greens to soups, stews and casseroles, as well as to herbal teas and coffee.

Another popular thing to forage in West Virginia then and now are edible mushrooms, including morels, shaggy mane, sulfur polypore, puff ball and chaaga. Out of the more than five thousand mushroom types in North America, only a few hundred are safe to eat. All mushrooms grow from a network of fine threads underneath the earth called the mycelium. They receive their nutrition from organic material. Native Americans ate raw mushrooms and roasted and dried them. They were also used in religious ceremonies and for medicinal uses. Native Americans used mushrooms to stop bleeding and treat diarrhea, dysentery and coughs. Early explorers and settlers also relied on mushrooms foraged from the forest. Mushroom hunting, especially the springtime ritual of morel hunting, is a time-honored tradition in the state. Mushrooms like to grow in old forests, and certain mushrooms tend to grow by certain trees. Interest in edible mushrooms is gaining popularity throughout the state, and an individual can join a foraging club to broaden their knowledge.

There are many delicious fruits that grow throughout the state, including strawberries, blackberries, blueberries, elderberries, wild grapes, crab apples, cranberries, huckleberries, cherries, dewberries and two very special to West Virginia: the pawpaw and persimmon. While their growing season and shelf life are relatively brief, even in modern times, the pawpaw was nonetheless prized by Native Americans and the settlers who followed them. Unique to the Appalachian region of the United States, the fruit tastes like a cross between a banana and a mango or a mango and avocado and has a creamy, tropical taste. Pawpaws (*Asimina triloba*) played an important part in the sustenance of the Native Americans and European settlers. Today, they are making a comeback and working their way back into the mainstream West Virginia diet. As they say, everything old becomes new again. There is a town in West Virginia named Paw Paw and a pawpaw festival. Being that it has a short shelf life and is hard to transport, it is not grown commercially in the United States. The fruit is not ripe or ready to eat until it looks rotten.

Another fruit found throughout West Virginia is the persimmon (*Diospyros virginiana*). Also known as the sugarplum, the persimmon tree averages

Left: This 1724 etching depicts Native Americans collecting sap from maple trees and boiling it down to syrup over an open fire. *Library of Congress.*

Right: This woodcut print created by West Virginia artist Eddie Maier, aka "Eddie Spaghetti," depicts the springtime arrival of some of West Virginia's native plants, including trillium, ramps and morels. *Author's collection.*

between thirty-five and sixty feet in height and has a distinctive craggy gray-black bark that resembles crocodile skin. They grow in old farm fields, woodland edges and floodplains, and the fruit are usually ripe in late autumn, when many people aren't thinking of fresh wild fruit. Like the pawpaw, persimmons don't travel well and have a short shelf life. The fruit is best after the first frost and can be eaten fresh or by freezing the pulp, which makes delicious jams, wine, ice cream and custard. The leaves can also be dried and used as a tea, which has a sassafras taste. Old-timers believe you can predict winter by cutting open a persimmon seed and looking at the shape of the kernel inside. If the kernel is spoon-shaped, expect plenty of snow to shovel. If it is fork-shaped, plan on a mild winter with powdery, light snow. If the kernel is knife-shaped, expect frigid winds that will "cut" like a blade.

The sugar maple tree (*Acer saccharum*) was another important food source in West Virginia's foodways, so much so that it is the official state tree. Native Americans made maple syrup and sugar by cutting or digging a hole into the bark of a sugar maple or birch tree. A wooden spout was inserted into the hole. As the sap ran out, it was collected in wooden containers and then boiled down over a fire in a large kettle for hours or maybe longer until the clear liquid turned a dark color. Maple sugar was also made by pouring the thickened liquid into molds and leaving it to harden.

In the modern age, refrigeration, sophisticated packaging, artificially extended growing seasons and cheap transportation of out-of-season foods from other countries, continents and even hemispheres have helped sever mankind's relationship with the seasons when it comes to food. Fresh strawberries in February? Sure. But for the majority of humanity's time on earth, that has definitely not been the case. When the connection to specific periods of harvesting is broken, so, too, are the accompanying traditions and celebrations. In West Virginia, however, there has remained a stubborn clinging to many of the old ways of gathering and preparing what nature has provided, and now those foods and traditions are being rediscovered. To the uneducated, the notion of seeking out native plants and animals may be daunting, to say the least. Obviously, one needs to learn not only to identify the native foods in question but also where they grow and when. Fortunately, there is a great body of information in books and online available to people with an interest in gathering natural foods of the region, and this information is based on experiences and practices that date back millennia.

❖ ❖ ❖

Nixtamalized Corn (Hominy), Mother Earth News

¼ cup pickling lime (food-grade calcium hydroxide)
3 quarts water
2 pounds clean, dried flour-corn kernels (about 1 quart)

Rinse the corn in a colander and set aside. In a large, stainless steel (nonreactive) pot, dissolve the lime in the water. Immediately wash off any lime that gets on your hands. Add the corn and discard any floating kernels. Bring to a boil over high heat. Reduce the heat to low and cook uncovered for 15 minutes. Turn off the heat, cool the pot and let it sit, uncovered, for 4 hours at room temperature or overnight in the refrigerator. Pour the corn into a colander in the sink. With the cold water running, rub the kernels between your hands to rub away the softened hulls (they will have a gelatinous texture). Rinse thoroughly (some old recipes say to wash between 4 and 11 times). Drain well. Use the whole, moist kernels in soups or stews. Or grind them through a food mill able to handle moist kernels to make masa, to which you can add enough water to make a slightly sticky dough for making tamales or, using a tortilla press, tortillas. Promptly refrigerate and use within 3 days.

❖ ❖ ❖

Baked Squash with Maple Syrup

3 acorn squash
1 teaspoon of salt
3 tablespoons of fat (butter, olive oil or bacon grease)

Preheat oven to 400 degrees. Put squash pieces, skin sides down, on a lightly greased rimmed baking sheet. Sprinkle with salt. Drizzle or add a little fat on each squash. Bake squashes until tender when pierced with a fork, about 40 minutes. Remove from oven and drizzle with local maple syrup. Keep warm until serving.

❖ ❖ ❖

Johnny Cakes

1 cup white cornmeal
1 teaspoon salt
1 cup boiling hot water
½ cup milk
3 tablespoons bacon drippings, butter or oil

In a medium bowl, combine the cornmeal and salt. Then slowly add the water and milk until it forms a thin batter that can be poured or spooned into a hot cast-iron skillet with hot fat. Be careful not to overcrowd the pan. Cook until golden on each side. Very good served with butter or with maple syrup.

Chapter 3
EARLY SETTLEMENTS

By being a part of the colony, and then state, of Virginia, West Virginia's history is tied to that of the mother state. Technically, that relationship dates all the way back to 1607, when a group of English gentlemen, with limited agricultural or survival skills, arrived in Jamestown to establish the first permanent English colony in what is now the United States. In that spirit, the state is also tied to earlier efforts, including the Lost Colony on Roanoke Island (in what is now North Carolina) and possibly to French trading villages established as far back as the seventeenth century. Certainly, there were French explorers, fur trappers and traders visiting the region far in advance of the settlers who were to follow the Jamestown colonization. Despite the many terrible calamities that Jamestown would endure over its first few decades of existence, it nonetheless served as the capital of Virginia for nearly eighty-three years, until Williamsburg assumed that role for another eighty-one years. In 1780, Richmond was chosen as the capital, and until West Virginia became its own state, the region's elected representatives had to make the long, hard journey over or around the mountains in order to take office. But there is a great deal of history to cover before that time.

For the first one hundred years of its existence, Virginia clung stubbornly to the navigable rivers feeding into the Chesapeake Bay. In 1630, after nearly twenty-five years of continuous settlement, the colony still only boasted around 2,500 settlers. Tobacco was king, and the rivers provided easy transport to market. There was little in the way of diversified agriculture, at least commercially, and despite the toll tobacco took on the soil, little effort was made to conserve or preserve land to sustain crops. Most plantations and farms acted as their own self-contained communities, able to provide their own services, such as woodworking or blacksmithing. This situation resulted in few significant towns and cities being developed, but even infrastructure, in the form of roads, was limited. When you compound this scenario with the natural impediment the mountains imposed—and the possibility of conflict with Native Americans beyond those mountains—it isn't hard to understand why it took so long for settlement, or even exploration, to occur in what is now West Virginia. The earliest known explorers, the aforementioned French traveling down from Canada, were of a culture interested only in furs and trade, not putting down roots on remote rivers like the Ohio and Monongahela. Even Native Americans had a more transient relationship with the region, maintaining more permanent villages in places like modern-day Ohio.

Slowly but surely, however, exploration did occur in the region. In 1669, a German physician named John Lederer visited the Blue Ridge Mountains and became the first European to enter what is now West Virginia, at the behest of the colony's government, in the hopes of finding a passage through the mountains. In 1671, explorers Thomas Batts and Robert Fallam traveled deep into the interior, as far as the falls of the Kanawha River. Perhaps the most pivotal moment of exploration, however, unfolded in 1716. Alexander Spotswood, governor of the Virginia Colony, wanted to push the boundaries of the western frontier in order to hopefully profit from land speculation and limit the French from encroaching by way of the Ohio River Valley. Spotswood mounted an expedition, composed of a group of wealthy men of Virginia, that crossed the Blue Ridge Mountains to the Shenandoah Valley. They explored the vast wilderness during the day, hunting game for sustenance along the way. In the evening, they exchanged stories, cooked the game they killed and drank champagne and other spirits. After they were safely home at the end of the expedition, Spotswood presented each member of the party with a golden horseshoe. On one side was a Latin inscription that read, "*Sic juvat transcendere montes*" or "thus he swears to cross the mountains." On the other side was written, "Order of the Golden Horseshoe." Because of this, the recipients became known as the Knights of the Golden Horseshoe. This expedition was an important factor in encouraging people to push through the established boundaries of the frontier, settling into present-day West Virginia.

By the early 1720s, settlers were creeping into what is now the eastern panhandle region. While the Potomac River was not nearly as friendly to river travel as others farther south, it nonetheless served as easier passage to an area that would develop as an important jumping-off point for settlers moving into the interior of the Mountain State. Over the next forty years or so, the move to colonize the region would grow thanks to settlers traveling down from eastern Pennsylvania to the Shenandoah Valley and beyond, including the legendary "Pennsylvania Dutch" (who were not Dutch at all but German); Quakers; descendants of the early settlers of Maryland, who were running out of land; and, perhaps most famously, the waves of Scots-Irish immigrants who were to gain a permanent foothold in the mountains of Appalachia and the pages of American history. Less famously, but sadly, the first African Americans were to enter the region as well, as slavery was legally observed and practiced in western Virginia, albeit to a much smaller degree than in Virginia proper. While each group brought with them their own customs and practices—and foodways—they all shared one constant reality: they would be moving into an area without the resources of civilization. If they wanted to eat, except for whatever supplies they could carry with them on primitive roads and trails over rugged terrain, they would have to hunt, fish, forage and grow the food themselves.

German immigrants came to the British colonies beginning around 1670 for reasons rooted in the religious conflicts that had developed between Catholicism and Protestantism and were compounded by the Thirty Years' War (1618–48). The opportunities for religious and political freedom, to escape disease and starvation and to acquire cheap available land proved enticing, particularly as so many of the Germans were farmers. By 1727, there was a German settlement called Mecklenburg, known today as Shepherdstown. German foods and foodways would ultimately loom large in West Virginia's future.

Permanent settlements continued to pop up in the eastern panhandle, like Bunker Hill, a Quaker community established near Berkeley Springs by Welsh immigrant Morgan Morgan and others. In addition to the natural inducements of abundant, uninhabited land, game and water, would-be settlers were offered even more motivation to colonize the lands beyond the Blue Ridge when, in 1730, the colonial government of Virginia offered speculators one thousand acres for each family that settled west of the mountains, with the stipulation that those recruited must come from outside Virginia, thus bolstering the colony's population as opposed to stretching it thin. More Germans arrived, as did a flood of Scots-Irish. There were

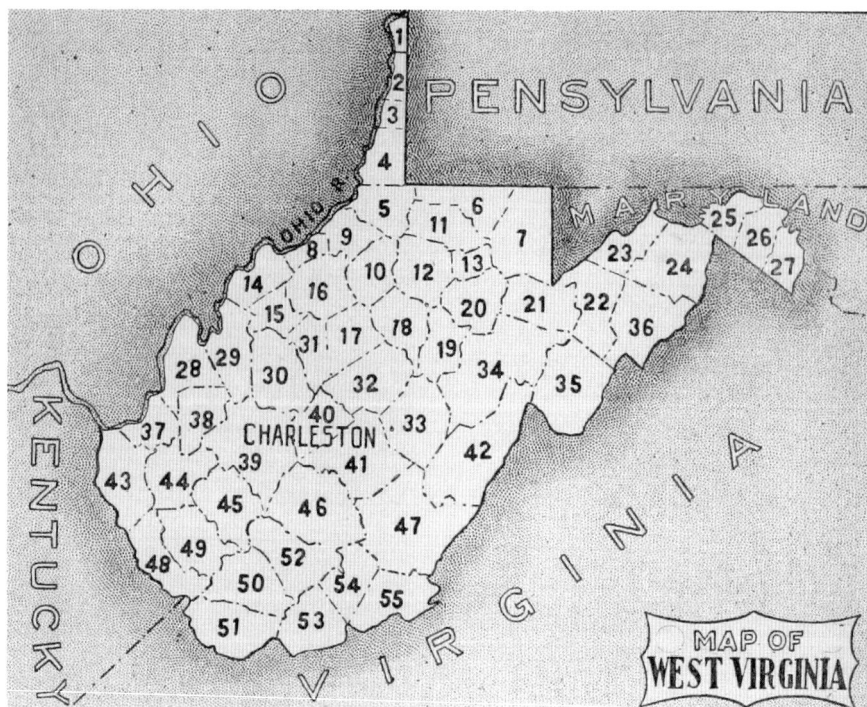

West Virginia became a state on June 20, 1863, after it seceded from Virginia. *Library of Congress.*

several approaches to settlement of western Virginia during the 1730s and 1740s. Some came northward, between the valley and the low country, following the Potomac and Shenandoah or up the James to its high-altitude headwaters and then over the mountain passes into the Greenbrier drainages. Others arrived from the west, having drifted down the Ohio River after passing through Pittsburgh, and opting to land and venture eastward into the interior. Others came north from Kentucky, including, at one point in time, the legendary Daniel Boone.

Many European settlers were attracted to the rugged mountains and a way of life that evolved far from the seat of government—and government regulation. By the middle of the eighteenth century, England had sent over fifty thousand people to America as punishment, most often for petty crimes such as hunting on land owned by the nobility. Convicts were shipped to Virginia and Maryland to work on large cotton and tobacco plantations owned by aristocratic families. The Scots-Irish had been subject to a campaign of war, conquest and exile at the hands of the English government for over a century. Most poignantly, many families had been ripped out of Scotland by the roots and transplanted to Northern Ireland, losing their ancestral lands. Once situated in the mountains of Appalachia, these immigrants and their descendants often practiced a lifestyle that deliberately avoided physical property in the form of large elaborate houses and dependencies in favor of property that was mobile—like pigs, for instance. Their experiences with the government-sanctioned seizing of lands and improvements bred a transient mindset and restless hunger to keep moving over the mountains.

Another impediment to settlement prior to the 1760s was the presence of the French and their Native American allies who jointly rendered life across the mountains less than desirable. Permanent settlements were established as early as the 1750s in the Greenbrier Valley and even as far north as Morgantown. But persistent Native American attacks hindered those efforts, and settlers were often forced to flee back across the mountains. It would not be until British forces, populated with a number of American colonial soldiers, defeated the French and took possession of Fort Duquesne, renaming it Fort Pitt, that meaningful attempts were made to settle into western Virginia. Fort Pitt became the city of Pittsburgh, from which settlement might more effectively be protected, although troubles between settlers and Native Americans would continue for another twenty-five years or so.

Morgantown represents a striking example of this shift in attempted settlement. Today a progressive city that is home to West Virginia University as well as other institutions and corporations of standing, Morgantown was at one time a far different community. Prior to the mid-eighteenth century, the area was the provenance of Native Americans and French traders. It was not until 1758 that Tobias Decker and a small party of settlers from the English colonies to the east ventured into present-day Monongalia County, settling an area along what is now known as Decker's Creek. It was a short-lived attempt, however, for the settlers were attacked by Delaware Indians in 1759, and the survivors fled back east. The Decker incident clearly illustrates the ongoing tensions between English colonists' desire for new land and the Native Americans and French who opposed that expansion. Those troubles, among others, led to the French and Indian War, and the resultant British victory revived efforts at expansion by the colonists. Colonel Zackquill Morgan arrived in the area around 1768 but did not attempt a permanent settlement until 1772. Ongoing trouble with the Native Americans compelled Colonel Morgan to initiate construction of a stockade fort for community protection and refuge in 1773. In 1785, the

Virginia Assembly granted a formal charter to the settlement, which came to be known as "Morgan's Town." Nearly thirty years elapsed between the first attempts to establish the town and its eventual legal recognition—proof that the path to settlement was usually long and arduous. In addition to the usual physical impediments facing pioneers, there was another enormous factor that affected settlement developing at a quicker pace: the Revolutionary War. The first battle fought in western Virginia occurred on October 10, 1774, at Point Pleasant.

Once the conflict between the colonies and the motherland reached the point of no return and true war broke out, among other actions, Great Britain ironically assumed the role the French had played, stirring up their Native American allies against settlers attempting to establish farms and communities west of Virginia and Maryland. This, in turn, led to the creation of stockades, blockhouses and forts throughout western Virginia. Local militia were created, and pioneer men went into service as soldiers, rangers and even spies seeking information on Native American movements and intentions.

Food supply was a major element in the outcome of the Revolutionary War. In Michael Lee Lanning's book *The American Revolution 100: The People, Battles and Events of the American Revolution*, he states:

> *In 1775, Congress approved food for soldiers at a per man per day ration of 1 lb. beef, or ¾ lb. pork, or 1 lb. salt fish, per day; 1 lb. bread or flour, half pint of rice or 1 pint of Indian meal and 1 quart of beer or cider per man per day. The men would also forage and hunt to supplement their diet. When in camp, the soldiers were placed in tents of six men called a mess and each man would take a turn at cooking.*

Even in the absence of British efforts to stir up Native American tribes against the settlers, there would no doubt have been conflict between the indigenous peoples and the pioneers, as history demonstrates repeatedly. Pontiac's Rebellion (1763), the French and Indian War (1754–63) and Lord Dunmore's War (1774) either arose from Native American anxiety due to colonial expansion or exacerbated those anxieties as a side effect of disputes between Great Britain and France. The core sticking point was possession of the land itself. Most Native Americans did not believe in the concept of private property and practiced communal land ownership. It could be said that much of what is now West Virginia functioned as an enormous "common" for Native Americans and that

The Point Pleasant Bridge located in Mason County was built in 1969 as a replacement for the collapsed Silver Bridge. The Battle of Point Pleasant was fought nearby. *Carol Highsmith Collection, Library of Congress.*

organized settlement in the area threatened hunting, gathering and the ability to move freely through the region. It isn't difficult to see how settlement threatened the status quo of Native American society in the region and that such a threat would be met with resistance. And the aggression was not limited to that resistance; the settlers themselves often initiated violence against the indigenous peoples, including Native Americans innocent of attacks on the settlements, as in the case of the massacre of Chief Logan's family in 1774 by Virginians.

When the inevitable conflicts did arise—or were at least threatened— settlers would "fort up," moving into whatever fortifications were constructed near their homes and relying on strength in numbers. That communal approach came in handy when it was time to harvest crops, although there was no guarantee of safety even then, as history has demonstrated.

When the Revolutionary War ended in 1783, the trickle of new settlers grew to a steady flow. New wagon roads were staked out and older ones improved, with routes leading into the area from Winchester and from established settlements in the Greenbrier Valley westward to the Kanawha River and the Ohio beyond. With the rise of settlement, the development of agriculture in the region began in earnest as well. German settlers, as well as Virginia Tidewater and Piedmont transplants, had already been farming in the eastern panhandle for decades by this point, and indeed, there were spots in that region of West Virginia that felt at home in Virginia proper or even Maryland or Pennsylvania. To the west, settlers were tasked with carving self-sustaining lives from the wilderness.

When would-be pioneers attempted to enter the region, they were forced to rely on paths that paralleled the waterways, animal trails that cut through the forests, Native American trails and a very few crude roads, all of which were established along paths of least resistance. A meaningful system of consistent overland transportation as we know it today did not exist. Settlers came first on foot, perhaps with packhorses, and then possibly with the addition of wagons. Regardless, transportation into the region was extremely time consuming, dangerous and uncomfortable. The crude paths, roads and river trails were at the mercy of the weather. If a stream or river was high after a storm, travelers had to choose between the risk of fording or the annoyance of waiting for the waters to recede. Conversely, conditions often rendered rivers too shallow to be depended on for river transport.

Prickett's Fort is the reconstruction of an eighteenth-century fort that settlers used as protection from Native American attacks. *Carol Highsmith Collection, Library of Congress.*

Early settlers walked or traveled on horseback with basic provisions, including just a few cooking utensils, often only a pot and skillet, which limited what dishes they might prepare. Often, they traveled with a milk cow, which provided milk for the children and carried some of the provisions needed on the long trek. But then, even if they had more in the way of cookware and utensils, the settlers would have been challenged in finding a wide variety of ingredients. Early settlers were often hungry and, until they could establish shelter and plant crops, were at the mercy of what they could forage and hunt from the land and water around them.

The first shelters were crude wigwam-type structures, hollowed-out trees or caves. The 1917 book *Marion County in the Making* details how the settlers might establish their homes:

After they cleared the land, they often constructed crude homes made from bark-covered, unhewn logs. The chinks were daubed with clay, and the roof was thatched with long grass and/or pine branches. The homes usually didn't have windows or chimneys. A fire burned on the dirt floor in the center of the room, and ventilation was not the best. Houses had only one living room—no kitchen, parlor or bedrooms at first. Also, shelter was needed for the oxen or horse, another for the chickens, a crib for corn or grain and a smokehouse for meats. All stock lived out on the open land, and fields for cultivation had to be fenced. Mostly, rails were used to make the old "worm fences."

There were no stoves yet, but in time, each home had a chimney with a "fireplace" (hearth) that served for heating, lighting and cooking. Cooking vessels, pots and pans were of cast iron; there was no graniteware or aluminum. There were some copper vessels and kettles. Glass and tin were scarce. There were a few porcelain cups, plates and bowls. Gourds were used for cups and bowls. In the absence of glass, greased cloth was used to let in light. A wooden shutter protected the window.

Much of the cooking was done in a Dutch oven, a large cast-iron pan with a cast-iron lid that could function somewhat like an oven. This Dutch oven was set on hot coals, and hot coals were placed on the lid. Skill was required to "set the oven" to get just the right amount of heat. They were cleaned by using corncobs and sand.

In time, a more substantial house may be constructed using logs that were cut square and did not require chinking. If a farmer was doing well, he may go one step further, constructing a house featuring a frame made from well-cut oak timbers that were braced together. The sides were covered with split-oak clapboards and the roof with cedar shingles, fastened down by wooden pegs and weighted with poles. A chimney made of clay or stone would be constructed at the end of the house.

Nails were scarce and sometimes could not be acquired. Often the boards needed to finish a log house were held in place by wooden pins. The boards of the roof were held down by placing log "riders" on them. The chimneys were constructed in a similar fashion as the house. Split sticks were placed across one another and plastered from the inside with clay to prevent the chimney from catching on fire. They were massive in size so they could accommodate the back logs.

Food was usually hard to come by in the first year, except for the meat they hunted. Even after they had successfully established their homesteads, most early settlers remained subsistence farmers, working their holdings on a small scale to supplement what they obtained in the wild, feed their family and maybe have a little extra to sell or trade. Given the difficulty of access to markets in the East or even along the Ohio to the west, there was not much motivation to invest in larger agricultural operations. Besides, game animals were plentiful. Hunting was essential to the survival of the settlers, particularly in the fall, after the leaves dropped but before heavy snow. Fall also was the time for butchering. Once they established a homestead, many settlers raised pigs that free ranged in the forests off mast. Once butchered and dried or salted, they not only provided food but also something to barter. As we have seen, foraging of native plants remained a key practice (as it continues to be to this day). In addition, streams and rivers were abundant with fish. Inevitably, however, hunting pressures led to a decrease in game populations, and permanent settlers turned increasingly to farming, if for no other reason than to establish reliable food sources from the garden, the field and in the form of livestock, as well as growing flax that could be woven into cloth.

Early on, housewives used baskets as a place to let their dough rise. Baskets were made of hickory splits woven together and had removable lids. The lid was placed on the basket, and then the basket was placed in a warm corner so the bread could rise. Butter bowls were made of sugar maple or gum trees. A wooden paddle was used for working the milk out of the butter. Cream was placed in a leather bag and then shaken and kneaded until butter was formed.

One way for food independence to occur was through the planting of fruit trees. As soon as the land was cleared and the ground was ready, settlers planted an orchard (pears, apples and peaches). It took a few years for the trees to bear fruit. In Jim Comstock's *The Hillbilly Bicentennial* book, he states that "settler Fleming Cobb planted apple and pear trees on his place near the mouth of Davis Creek in Kanawha County. He brought the plantings from Virginia in his saddle bag."

Even the legendary Johnny Appleseed (real name John Chapman) passed through the northern panhandle, leaving fledgling orchards in his wake. To this day, the eastern panhandle maintains a strong presence of large commercial apple orchards. Obviously, the determination of settlers to establish fruit trees early as a food source makes sense. But apples held perhaps an even stronger allure: they could be turned into hard cider, which prior to the rise of beer in the mid-nineteenth century was the light alcoholic drink of choice in America. Fermented cider assured the drinker he was ingesting something that was purified by alcohol as opposed to some questionable or contaminated water source, and everyone, including men, women and children, drank hard cider daily. The reality of it is that, then as now, life can be hard, and the relief provided by alcohol is much sought after. Cider vinegar was also an important part of life for the early settlers, as it served as a pickling agent for them to preserve food. Another important crop favored by the settlers, albeit not a perennial one, was the same one revered by Native Americans, as noted before: corn.

Corn was the most commonly used grain throughout Appalachia for several reasons. First, there was its versatility. Corn could be ground into meal or served as roasting ears, hominy, mush and dozens of other dishes. It also provided livestock feed and could be dried and stored. And like the apple, it could be converted to hard alcohol—and thus was easier to transport to market. Corn liquor represented perhaps West Virginia's first value-added product. But more on that later.

Then there was corn's reliability. It thrived in harsh environments, offered a high ratio of yield versus seeds-sown and was easy to store. Generally, as soon as a prospective settler cleared a patch of land, he would plant corn, ensuring a food source to get him through the hard times of winter.

Finally, corn represented a way to gain landownership. Land grants often hinged on settlers' construction of a cabin and the raising of a crop of grain. Meeting those two standards entitled the settler to four hundred acres of land and a preempted right to one thousand acres or even more. This model followed the original "tomahawk" rights approach of gaining land by clearing trees on a desired property and then cutting the initials on the trees left standing.

In addition to corn's appeal to the settlers, it also directly contributed to the beginnings of infrastructure, communities and economy on the frontier for the simple reason that in order to reach some of its potential, it must be processed in the form of grinding. As noted in the last chapter, prior to the influx of settlers from the East into western Virginia, Native Americans had long been operating their own crude mortar and pestles throughout the region, indeed in most regions where corn was grown and consumed. Being over one hundred miles from the nearest organized settlements meant that the early settlers had to process corn as best they could—usually with a mortar and pestle not unlike the Native Americans before them. Simple tin graters were also used to grind the corn. After graters, hand mills became popular. The mill consisted of two large round stones. The larger stone was placed on the floor in a stationary position; the upper stone, called the "runner," was moved around by a pole attached to a beam in the ceiling. The corn was placed in a small opening in the top of the runner, and the meal found its way out through a hole in the hoop that encircled the stones.

But with large families and growing numbers of settlers arriving, it inevitably came time to process larger amounts of corn (and, later, wheat and other grains), and that meant the development of larger milling operations in the form of a gristmill. These mills were situated along waterways that were dammed up to create a millpond. Using the energy inherent in the water's movement to move gears that in turn moved a grinding stone that would crush corn into powder or cornmeal, the rise of the gristmill generally not only represented the earliest industry in a settled area but also served as a social hub. This also marked a transition in a diet that relied heavily on corn and bread. In many instances, other services and, eventually, communities would develop around the mill. If folks were going to be spending time at the mill waiting on their corn to be processed, it only made sense for enterprising individuals to establish public houses or dry goods stores or blacksmith shops nearby. Gristmills were also an important factor in the growth of a market economy because they connected the product to the market.

As small communities began to evolve around mills, crossroads or other logical sites that encouraged the establishment of towns, it was only natural that taverns and inns would also begin to appear. In his landmark multi-volume series of books on the history of Monongalia County, the late Dr. Earl Core references earlier historians to provide some useful insights into the region's taverns. Quoting historian Oliver Perry Chitwood, he notes, "Every county seat in Virginia had a tavern, which served as the political and social center of the community….The amusements…were not always harmless… for gambling as well as drinking was encouraged." Dr. Core further reprints (from James Morton Callahan's *Semi-centennial History of West Virginia*) a list of tavern rates for food, drink and lodging, as directed by the Randolph County court in 1788, including:

> *Madeira wine, per half pint 25 cents*
> *Other wines, per half pint 20 ⅚ cents*
> *West India Rum, per half pint 16⅔ cents*
> *Other rums, per half pint 12½ cents*
> *Peach brandy, per half pint 11¹⁄₁₉ cents*
> *Good whiskey, per half pint 11¹⁄₁₉ cents*
> *Dinner 16⅔ cents*
> *Breakfast 12½ cents*
> *Supper 12½ cents*
> *Lodging, in clean sheets each night 8½ cents*

Apparently, a detailed list of the varieties of alcohol was of more importance to the clientele than any specifics regarding the food itself.

Domesticated livestock represented another aspect of food independence, certainly among Scots-Irish pioneers. In addition to their cultivation of pigs, as noted earlier, the Scots-Irish often traveled with cows, as they depended heavily on milk for nutrition. Along with a reputation for being hot-tempered, clannish and fiercely independent, the Scots-Irish brought their farming and herding culture with them into undeveloped regions, notably practicing the "commons" method of grazing, wherein they allowed the cattle to roam freely on the hillsides on a communal plot of land even as their pigs ranged freely in the forests, fattening on acorns, hickory nuts and the all-important chestnut. The Scots-Irish also brought the arts of whiskey making, weaving and folk ballads and the use of flax. But about those pigs…

Pigs have been in America longer than the Pilgrims of New England— first arriving in Jamestown in 1608—and the influence of pork is still profound on the cuisine of the southern United States, including West Virginia. As is explored at length by David Hackett Fischer in his indispensable book *Albion's Seed*, inhabitants of specific regions of the United Kingdom tended to migrate to specific regions of the colonies, so, for example, settlers in early Tidewater Virginia tended to come from one part of England, while New England transplants were primarily from another. Therefore, the various practices and behaviors they engaged in in the old country often took root in the New World. Food and food preparation methods were no exception to this phenomenon, as the Scots-Irish experience makes clear. Their commitment to pork and, perhaps most notably, the tendency to prepare pork through frying, as they and their ancestors had done in Scotland, Northern Ireland and the border regions of northern England, absolutely contributed to the popularity of fried foods in the South. They also tended to emphasize simpler dishes, cooking styles and ingredients. When you consider that by 1790, residents of Scots-Irish origin had already swollen to represent 11 percent of Virginia's population, it's no wonder their impact would be felt on cuisine, as well as other aspects of society. Of course, all pioneers, regardless of their heritage, would gravitate toward simpler dishes and methods of preparations given the overwhelming number of tasks facing them if they were to survive, much less prosper.

As we have observed, when the pioneers arrived at the lands they had chosen to improve, there was no house or cabin waiting for them. There certainly was no kitchen. Cooking took place over an open campfire. Soup and one-pot meals became common because they had so much work to do that they needed something that could cook all day while they worked clearing land, hunting, putting in gardens and tending to them and building homes. Such meals also stretched further and fed more people. Dried food (beans, pumpkins and squash) were an important part of the settlers' diets, as they had been to the Native Americans before them. The tradition of a big pot of soup beans simmering on the stove continues in many West Virginia homes to this day, sometimes consisting of heirloom beans long forgotten by the average American consumer but remembered and preserved by conscientious individuals with a strong connection to their heritage (or rediscovered by a growing number of modern folks interested in the diversity and often superior tastes these nearly lost varieties represent).

Even when cabins and fireplaces were constructed, the settlers continued to cook food over a flame in an open hearth over logs held by andirons. Cast-iron kettles and pots were suspended on S-shaped hooks over the flames. Food was served in wooden or metal bowls. Given the rigors of traveling into the wild, the notion of transporting great numbers of cast-iron cookware, dishes, plates and so on would have been difficult, and most pioneers were limited to what they had to work with until communities and stores were established. They had only the basics with them. Once these families established an agricultural environment and improved their quality of life, they were able to import extra plates, bowls, cups, utensils and other kitchenware. They also eventually incorporated ceramics into the preparation, storage and consumption of food.

While it is tempting to romanticize the frontier lifestyle, the truth is life was hard and conditions could be very harsh. As previously mentioned, early settlers were often hungry. The family garden or "truck patch" was usually planted with potatoes, squash, corn and beans, and when it came time to harvest in the fall, there was often an abundance. But the challenge of storing food through the long winter, as well as the absence of fresh greens, certainly affected the situation, and by spring, with stored provisions running out and a new garden not yet producing, families could find themselves in dire straits. This scenario would compel settlers to perfect storage methods and, in time, gain access to salt, which would enable them to cure meats for long-term storage.

Even with a garden planted in the spring, the settlers faced uncertainty. In his book *Historical Sketches of Pocahontas County, West Virginia* (1901), author William T. Price discussed the challenges of producing viable crops, specifically all-important corn:

> *Killing frosts early and late made the working land a precarious source of subsistence until a comparatively recent period in the history of our county. As late as 1810, the fact that corn would ripen at Marlin's Bottom enough to be fit for a meal was a years' wonder. Gardens for onions, parsnips, cucumbers, pumpkins, and turnips; patches for buckwheat, corn, beans and potatoes for many years comprised most of the pioneer farming enterprise in the way of supplementing their supplies of game and fish. The implements used for clearing and cultivating these gardens and truck patches were of home manufacture and for the most part rather rudely constructed, as mere makeshifts are apt to be.*

Price illustrates his point with a specific story:

> *About 1810, Major William Poage, then living at Marlin's Bottom (now Marlington), had a field of corn near the mouth of the creek that was looking very promising. He was asked by a neighbor how much corn fit for bread did he think he might have from that splendid looking field. Major Poage, after some thoughtful hesitation, replied very cautiously that he ventured to think there was a probability of there being eight to ten bushels. This was spoken of the marvel of the season, that out of three or four hundred bushels of corn raised at Marlin's Bottom, there might be eight or*

ten fit for bread, johnnycakes, pone and hoecake, and happy people thought things now looked like living.

The much-celebrated desire for religious freedom that is so often ascribed to colonial Americans (and subsequent generations) would probably not be very apparent on the frontier. The early settlers were too busy trying to survive from day to day. But clergymen like "Bishop" Francis Asbury were eager to spread the gospel throughout West Virginia during those hard early years and have left behind some written accounts that help paint a clearer picture of what life was like among the pioneers. In Core's *Monongalia Story*, Asbury's diary of a 1788 preaching mission that took him from North Carolina up through what is now Greenbrier County and into the Tygart Valley is quoted and repeatedly details the hardships and deprivations he encountered among the settlers of western Virginia, even in June:

> *Our course lay over mountains and through valleys, and the mud and the mire were such as might scarcely be expected in December. We came to an old forsaken habitat in Tyger's Valley. Here our horses grazed while we boiled our meat….We journeyed on through devious lonely wilds, where no food might be found, except what grew in the woods, or was carried with us.*

On one occasion, all Asbury had for supper was tea, with no feed for the horses. To add insult to injury, when he preached in Morgantown, he encountered "a lifeless, disorderly people….It is a matter of grief to behold the excesses, particularly in drinking, which abound here." One shudders to think how the good Bishop Asbury would react to the "excesses" of a WVU football game tailgate!

Even into the 1790s, West Virginia's settlers still had issues with Native Americans, not to mention other natural calamities. In 1790, the Upper Ohio Valley had an early frost in the fall, and as a result, people had to harvest their corn crops before it was dried and ready to gather. The undried corn made several people very ill. Even the livestock got sick from eating the bad corn, and there weren't many cows, oxen and pigs to begin with. To complicate matters, Native Americans had slaughtered or driven out the game in the woods in order to harass the settlers. It was a dark time for the region. It would not be until the Treaty of Greenville and the subsequent marking of boundaries between Native American territory and lands open to European American settlers that hostilities between the settlers and Native Americans would end.

Amid their hardships, however, the early settlers nonetheless still managed to find enjoyment, camaraderie and celebration, and perhaps nowhere is that more evident than in marriage ceremonies. In his celebrated book *Notes on the Settlement and Indian Wars of the Western Parts of Virginia and Pennsylvania*, Joseph Doddridge described nuptial celebrations on the frontier:

> *The ceremony of the marriage preceded the dinner, which was substantial backwoods feast of beef, pork, fowls, and sometimes venison and bear meat roasted and boiled, with plenty of potatoes, cabbage and other vegetables. During the dinner the greatest of hilarity always prevailed; although the table might be a large slab of timber, hewed out with a broad ax, supported by four sticks set in auger holes; and the furniture, some old pewter dishes and plates and the rest, wooden bowls and trenches; a few pewter spoons, much battered around the edge, were to be seen at some tables. The rest were made of horns.*
>
> *Pretty late in the night someone would remind the couple must stand in the need of refreshment; black Betty, which was the name of the bottle was called for and sent up the ladder, but beef, pork and cabbage sent along with her as would afford a good meal for a half dozen hungry men. The young couple was compelled to eat and drink, more or less, of whatever was offered them.*

Back beyond the mountains, in the long-settled areas that hugged the Atlantic seaboard, progress was coming, in the form of the earliest days of the Industrial Revolution, the slowly growing confidence of American government and the general standard of living, which included culinary improvements and even luxuries. *American Cookery* by Amelia Simmons, considered the first American cookbook, was published in 1796. The more accessible areas of the eastern panhandle were beneficiaries of this progress, as witnessed in the growth and relative prosperity of towns like Harpers Ferry and Shepherdstown. By the 1780s, the town of Bath (now Berkeley Springs) could even boast of the United States' first spa, centered on the area's natural mineral springs that had been celebrated since prehistoric times and patronized by no less than George Washington himself. But in the thinly settled mountainous region between old Virginia and the Ohio River, such progress was largely absent. There was still much work to be done.

❖ ❖ ❖

Hardtack

Hardtack, also called sea biscuits, are unleavened bread or crackers that have been made and eaten since ancient times. It has kept explorers, soldiers and settlers into West Virginia nourished and alive due to its long shelf life. It will keep if you keep it dry.

5 cups flour
3 teaspoons salt
1 cup water

Preheat oven to 375 degrees. Combine flour with salt in a mixing bowl. Gradually add water and mix with hands until the dough comes together. Roll out on a table to about ½-inch thickness. Use a knife to cut dough into nine equal square pieces. Place on baking sheet and use a nail to make 16 evenly spaced holes (4x4 pattern) in each square, then turn over to the other side, being careful not to poke all the way through the dough. Bake for 30 minutes and then turn over and bake another 30 minutes. Cool on a rack in a dry room.

❖ ❖ ❖

Stew

½ cup flour
2 teaspoons salt
½ teaspoon black pepper
3 pounds venison or beef roast, cubed in 1-inch pieces
3 tablespoons vegetable oil
3 tablespoons red wine vinegar
1 cup wine
5 cups beef broth
2–3 bay leaves
3 large potatoes, peeled and diced
2 onions, chopped
3 cloves garlic, chopped
3 celery stalks with leaves chopped
5 carrots, diced

Combine the flour, salt and pepper in a bowl, add the venison or beef and toss to coat well. Heat 3 teaspoons of the oil in a large pot. Add the beef a few pieces at a time; do not overcrowd. Cook, turning the pieces, until beef is browned on all sides, about 5 minutes per batch; add more oil as needed between batches.

Remove the beef from the pot and add the vinegar and wine. Deglaze the pan over medium-high heat for a few minutes, scraping the bits off the bottom of the pan. Add the beef, beef broth and bay leaves. Bring to a boil, then reduce to a slow simmer.

Cover and cook until the beef is tender, about 1½ hours. Add the potatoes and simmer until vegetables are tender, about 30 minutes. Add the onions, garlic, celery and carrots and simmer, covered, for 10 minutes. Add broth or water if the stew is dry. Season with salt and pepper to taste.

❧ ❧ ❧

Dandelion Greens

3 pounds dandelion greens
5 strips fried bacon
5 cloves garlic
½ teaspoon hot pepper flakes
Pinch of freshly grated nutmeg
Salt and pepper to taste

Cook greens in a large pot of boiling salted water (3 tablespoons salt for 8 quarts), uncovered, until ribs are tender, about 10 minutes. Drain in a colander, then rinse under cold water to stop cooking and drain well, gently pressing out excess water.

Fry bacon in a heavy skillet over medium heat until crispy. Remove bacon but leave grease. On medium-low heat, cook garlic until softened. Do not burn. Add the hot pepper flakes and freshly grated nutmeg. Increase heat to medium-high, then add greens and sea salt and sauté until coated with oil and heated through, about 4 minutes. Throw bacon in right before you serve it. This can also be made a vegetarian dish by omitting bacon and using ½ cup olive oil.

❖ ❖ ❖

Mrs. Hall's Salt Rising Bread

In the evening—peel a medium-sized potato. Grate in a bowl. Add two heaping tablespoons of cornmeal, 1 teaspoon of salt and 1 tablespoon of sugar. Pour 1 pint boiling water over mixture and mix well. Pour in a quart jar or bigger. Set jar in a vessel of very warm water with water deep enough to equal the depth of the jar. Set container on stove. The next morning, there should be a head on top of the liquid (if not, it is no good and you must start over). Pour liquid into bowl adding ½ teaspoon of baking soda. Mix in 2½ cups of flour to make batter and set in a warm place. When light and spongy, put 9 cups of flour in a large bowl. Add 2 cups of hot water, 2 tablespoons of sugar, 1 teaspoon salt and ⅓ cup of lard. Add the sponge and mix well. If needed, add a little more flour to make a medium stiff dough. Knead well. Place in a well-greased pan. Let rise until double the size. Bake in 375-degree oven for 40 to 45 minutes.

Chapter 4

EXPANDING SETTLEMENTS, INFRASTRUCTURE AND INDUSTRY

The settlement of West Virginia advanced much in the way a river behaves when it encounters a large rock—by simply swirling around and past it. For the vast interior of the region, that is precisely what occurred. Certainly, there were efforts at settlement deep into the mountains at times. In the more accessible regions of western Virginia, towns and cities would grow and boast of schools, churches, newspapers, physicians and much of what would pass for a modern, progressive town throughout the first one hundred years or so of the nation's history. But the tide of immigrants moved quickly westward, taking advantage of the Ohio River from the north and east and other avenues from the south.

The state's distinctive regions rendered each different from the other in significant ways, not least in the founding of industry. Very early in the settlement of western Virginia, one industry was established or, more accurately, developed as an extension of earlier Native American activities and was directly tied to food. This industry was to flourish for over a century and is making something of a comeback in the present day: salt making.

Salt was an important commodity on the frontier. As settlers moved away from the coast and settled in the vast western Virginia wilderness, they started looking for salt sources to preserve food. They followed animals to salt licks and would start settlements close to these salt deposits. But ultimately, salt deposits were discovered in the Kanawha River Valley. Fed by the remains of an ancient ocean hundreds of feet below the surface, these deposits led to large-scale industrial salt-mining operations, which would in time grow into a powerful exporter in the global marketplace.

Throughout the early days of settlement, there was little money in the mountains, and pioneers often had to barter for supplies. That situation was exacerbated after the Revolution, given the fact that Continental money generated by the new government of the United States was practically worthless. If settlers wanted to be able to acquire certain goods or services, trade or barter might well prove the only way to achieve that. Salt represented a very valuable commodity, much in demand, and an ideal asset for trading. When settlers had access to salt, they would often pack their canoes and rafts with it (and other supplies) to trade for items such as rope, butter, oil, farm products and sometimes manufactured products from more developed regions in the established eastern areas in both the colonial and post-Revolution eras.

Mary Draper Ingles was the first white woman to see the valleys of West Virginia and the first to harvest salt, although neither of those events occurred of her own free will. In 1755, Ingles was taken captive by Native Americans and forced to walk hundreds of miles into the wilderness. Among other things, she was compelled to harvest salt for her captors near the modern-day border of Ohio, Kentucky and West Virginia. She eventually escaped her kidnappers and, improbably, made her way home. Not surprisingly, so did her knowledge of the presence of the salt, although significant exploitation of the tremendous salt deposits in the Kanawha Valley was still decades away.

Joseph Ruffner started the first salt-making operation along the Kanawha River in Malden and called it "Kanawha Red." The Kanawha River was relatively navigable near the salt deposits and drained directly into the Ohio River, so it was only natural that traders and marketers of salt would take advantage of the sort of water transportation that eluded the majority of western Virginia. The first boats that transported salt were raft-like dugouts carved out of poplar trees. As the demand for salt increased and the industry expanded, these small rafts could not handle the trade. Flatboats, which were already hard at work up and down the mighty Ohio, took their place and increased the number of barrels of salt that could be transported. As is often the case, the rise of one industry fueled others: salt making fed the salt trade, which fed boat building, which required timber. Just the sort of situation that gave rise to the cliché "a rising tide lifts all boats."

In time, with the development of powered machines throughout the nineteenth century, the scale of operations grew. The *West Virginia Encyclopedia* provides a brief overview of the salt-making process:

Shallow wells reached the subterranean brine water. Steam engines pumped the salty water from one or more wells to an elevated tank. From that point, water ran as needed into the evaporator, a giant flat pan heated by steam. As the brine evaporated, its salt crystallized. Workers skimmed the salt onto drain boards. After a period, the salt was lifted and wheeled to a storage house where it was packed into barrels for shipment.

With expanding settlement, the need for salt increased, and so did the salt industry. The Kanawha Salines became one of the most lucrative and important salt manufacturers in the United States. Salt was shipped along the Ohio and Monongahela Rivers up to the Allegheny River and on to Lake Erie.

Salt making may no longer be the large-scale industry that it once was in West Virginia, but it is making a comeback of sorts. Seventh-generation salt makers (and siblings) Nancy Bruns and Lewis Payne have revived a family business that dates to 1817: J.Q. Dickinson Salt-Works. Located in Malden, West Virginia, their business is situated at the heart of the once-thriving Kanawha Valley salt industry (and is well worth visiting). In their words, they are working "to produce a rare, small-batch finishing salt, harvested from the ancient Iapetus Ocean trapped underneath the mountains of Appalachia."

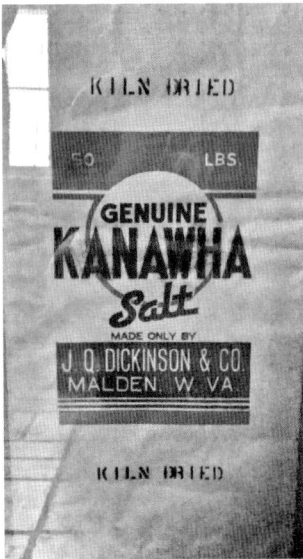

J.Q. Dickinson Salt-Works, located in Malden, West Virginia, has roots that stretch back to 1817. It is considered a specialty food item and is in high demand throughout the state due to its high quality and local roots. *J.Q. Dickinson.*

As has been noted, western Virginia—or at least that portion of it that lay beyond the mountains—never developed the plantation culture that is closely identified with Virginia proper and, as a result, did not have a large population of African American slaves. The salt industry, however, was an exception in that it employed slave labor to meet demand, part of a long, tragic pattern of human trafficking in support of commerce. In 1619, the first African American slaves were brought into Virginia by Dutch traders. By 1665, there were still fewer than 500 Africans in the colony, as colonists depended instead on indentured servants primarily of British

Salt has played an important role in West Virginia foodways since prehistory. After the Civil War, many free African Americans came to West Virginia to work in the salt industry. *Library of Congress.*

descent for the simple reason that importing indentured servants rewarded the owners with land grants. After several years, those indentured servants would be free from indenture and begin to claim and work their own lands. Some of them would become wealthy in their own right. In those early decades, the indentured servants often worked in the fields alongside the enslaved African Americans. During the 1660s, as Europeans began to venture off the plantations westward in search of their own land, demand for slave labor grew, and the slave trade flourished. By 1750, there were over 250,000 slaves working throughout the southern colonies—almost 40 percent of the total population.

As people ventured westward into western Virginia, they settled on smaller farms that did not require slaves. The thin soils of mountainous terrains would not support the vast fields of tobacco for which Virginia was famous, and therefore, slave labor was not in demand. The typical subsistence farms grew only what the family needed to get by or barter with. To be sure, there were larger farms in the South Branch, Greenbrier, Monongahela and Kanawha Valleys that resembled the large tobacco (and other cash crop) operations back across the mountains and used slaves, but their numbers were relatively few.

Plantation agriculture in Virginia began to decline in the 1800s, particularly as the soil was worn out from decades of tobacco cultivation. This, combined with a demand for slave labor in the cotton-growing South, rendered slavery much less profitable in Virginia. Slaves were frequently hired out or sold to the cotton plantation owners in the Deep South.

There did remain some demand for slave labor in western Virginia, courtesy of the salt industry, which was driven by poor white transients and slave labor, often leased from eastern Virginia. Of the slaves in the Kanawha Valley, half were owned or hired by salt firms. Of these, 40 percent were used to mine coal to power steam engines for the salt works because they could be hired from their owners for much lower wages than white laborers demanded. These slaves were usually leased and insured, rather than bought, due to the risk of death or injury in the coal mines. By 1850, salt makers along the Kanawha River employed 1,500 slaves. They held various occupations, including coal miners, teamsters, kettle tender, steam engine tender, salt lifter, wheelers, general laborers, packers, blacksmiths, foremen, farmers and cooks. Slaves were often leased from eastern Virginia.

The African Americans contributed to West Virginia's culinary history not only through their forced labor at the saltworks. They also brought with them foodways that survived the horrific transport from their homelands on the African continent and indelibly made their mark on southern culinary traditions—including West Virginia's. Yams, cucumbers and watermelons were all introduced by African Americans to the culture at large. It should be noted that even on the large plantations to the east, slaves were expected to keep their own gardens to augment their food. Native Americans and African Americans had a complex relationship, sometimes living side by side and intermarrying and sometimes being returned to their captors for a ransom.

While salt reflected perhaps the first centralized industry to export consistently outside the borders of present-day West Virginia, there was another example of an industry that was common to most every region, although its clientele was more local in nature. Perhaps not surprisingly, the key ingredient driving that industry was the mainstay crop of corn. Enterprising residents on the frontier began manufacturing the original "value-added product" of its time—"value-added" meaning a commodity or ingredient that could be transformed or refined or, in this instance, distilled into a new product that was more marketable, easier to transport, in demand and thus more valuable: corn liquor or, as it is more commonly referred to, "moonshine."

The process of distilling alcohol from corn was not a particularly difficult one. Of course, know-how was important, and there was some modest investment needed in the necessary equipment. But in the big picture, the process was not that complicated, and the raw materials needed to make moonshine were minimal: corn, water, yeast, malt (often barley), sugar and, depending on your legal situation, some privacy. First you create the mash, a slurry of corn, barley, water and yeast. Once cooked and cooled, the mash sits in an airtight container to ferment for several weeks. Afterward, it's introduced to the still, which collects the ethanol vapor produced by the reheated mash. The vapor then condenses, and moonshine is created— ready for your mason jar of choice.

Corn liquor's nickname, "moonshine," was perhaps inspired by distillers' tendency to work in secret, often by the light of the moon, to avoid law enforcement. *Library of Congress.*

By using high and low tunnels that help extend the growing season, the West Virginia Department of Agriculture is hoping the strawberry will become a specialty crop. *West Virginia Department of Agriculture.*

March 19, Maple Day in West Virginia, is when the state's maple producers like the Flanigan family open to the public for tasting, education and purchasing. *West Virginia Department of Agriculture.*

Soup beans and bloody butcher cornbread. *Author's collection.*

Glade Creek Mill, located in Babcock State Park in Fayette, West Virginia, is a living monument to the over five hundred mills that once were located throughout the state. *Carol Highsmith Collection, Library of Congress.*

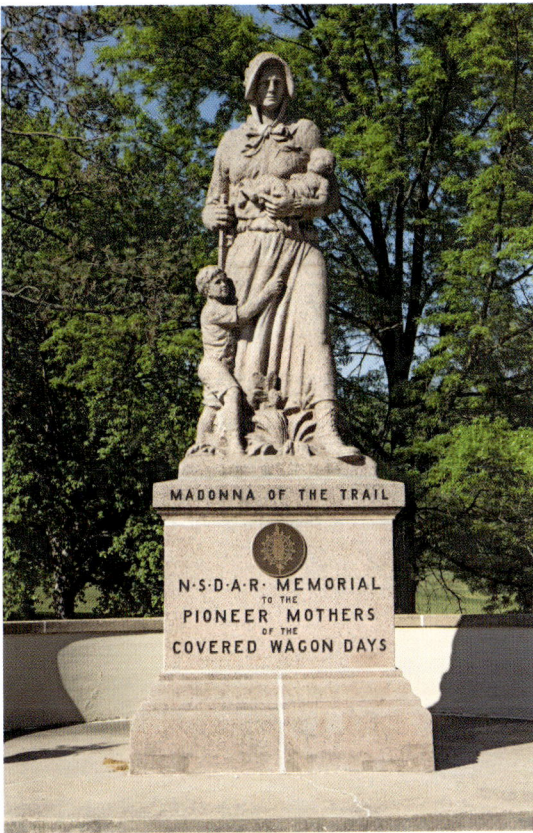

Left: Route 40, formerly the National Road in Wheeling, is known as gateway to the West. The Madonna statue honors the women who endured the hardships of pioneering the way west. *Carol Highsmith Collection, Library of Congress.*

Below: Dolly Sods is a high-altitude plateau that is more like a Canadian landscape than West Virginia and a great place to go berry picking. *Jay Mahoney.*

The New River Bridge represents a very tangible example of efforts to overcome the state's challenging topography and subsequent issues with mass transportation into and out of the interior regions of the state. *Library of Congress.*

Cooper's Rock is a favorite tourist destination with a magnificent virgin hemlock trail to hike. These trees are an important factor in the survival of trout, birds and mammals. *Judy Lochner.*

In 1927, Pocahontas County farmers grew one hundred bushels of potatoes an acre. Using today's technology, farmers are hoping to grow three hundred bushels an acre. *Carol Highsmith Collection, Library of Congress.*

Above: Legend states that in 1753, the Native Americans had planted fields of pumpkins along the Potomac River and a great flood occurred, causing the "Year of the Great Pumpkin Flood." *Carol Highsmith Collection, Library of Congress.*

Left: Morel mushrooms are a spring delicacy in West Virginia. They usually appear sometime in April, around the start of spring gobbler season. *Justin Vance.*

Above: A ramp patch in Preston County. Ramps tend to grow beneath the canopies of beech, poplar, maple, oak and hickory trees. They spring up before the tree canopy shades over the area. *Author's collection.*

Right: The pawpaw, also known as the "West Virginia banana," is North America's largest native fruit. *Justin Vance.*

Left: The golden delicious apple is the state fruit of West Virginia. The beautiful sweet yellow apple was discovered in Clay County. *Author's collection.*

Below: From a large garden, square foot beds or pots outside, growing your own food is an old-time tradition in the Mountain State. *Author's collection.*

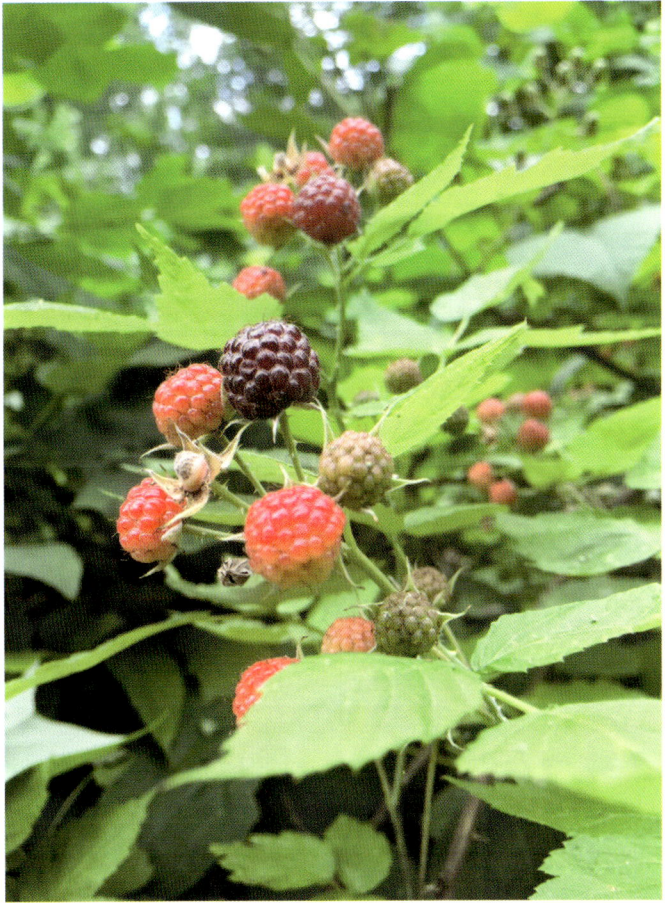

Right: In folklore, blackberries were once believed to protect families against vampires because they would become distracted by counting all the berries. *Author's collection.*

Below: Trout is a favorite food in West Virginia, especially pan-fried outside after a day of fishing. In 1973, West Virginia designated the brook trout as the state fish. *Jay Mahoney.*

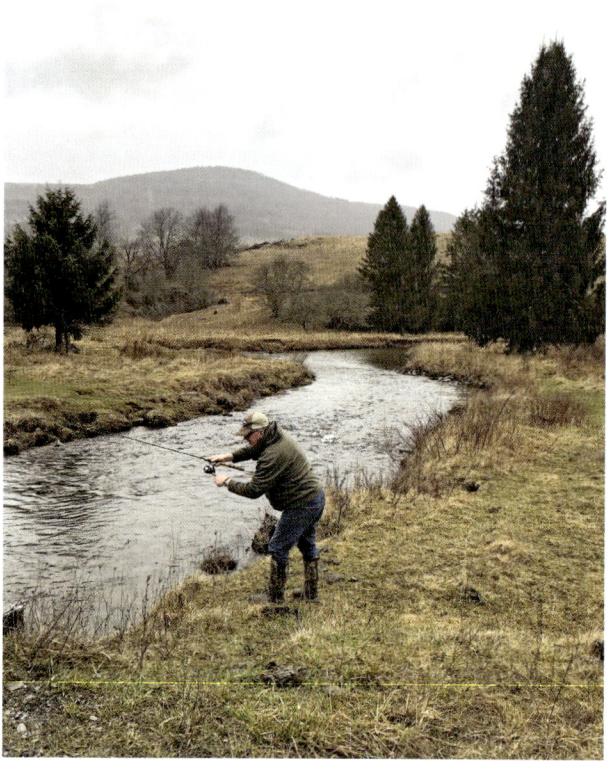

Right: Trout fishing is a favorite pastime in West Virginia, and the DNR stocks over 150 bodies of water throughout the state. *Jay Mahoney.*

Below: Tailgating may not have been born in West Virginia, but it has certainly been raised to an art form here, like this duck pastrami created by chef Jay Mahoney. *Jay Mahoney.*

Cooking outside over an open fire was a necessity for Native Americans and early settlers. Today, many people still cook over a fire, but for fun, usually not necessity. *Author's collection.*

Left: Hawk Knob Cidery and Meadery located in Lewisburg, West Virginia, handcrafts all its cider and mead. *Author's collection.*

Below: The Feast of the Seven Fishes Festival Cucina is a cooking school with the goal of preserving and sharing Italian American Christmas Eve foodways for future generations. *Addie Glotfelty.*

FESTIVAL CUCINA

EAST *of the* SEVEN FISHES

Right: The wedding cookie table originated in southwestern Pennsylvania and eastern Ohio but has become a wedding tradition in West Virginia. *Author's collection.*

Below: Sorghum cane is fed into a machine that squeezes out the liquid that is eventually boiled down to make molasses. *West Virginia Department of Agriculture.*

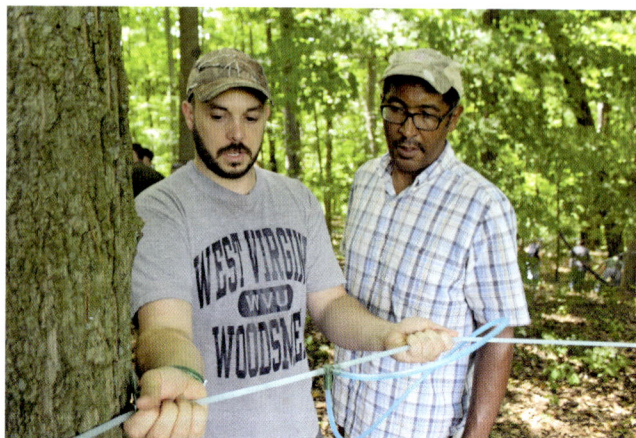

Rich Flanigan, of Flanigan Family Maple, and Philip Lee learn the basics of maple syrup during "Maple Camp" at West Virginia University. *West Virginia Department of Agriculture.*

Historically, West Virginia's cooking is a mixture of what was available and economical. Most families had pork, milk and flour for sausage gravy and biscuits. *Author's collection.*

West Virginia farmers' markets provide fresh, local produce, economic opportunities for farmers and a place for people to gather and socialize. *Author's collection.*

Right: Chestnuts were used in many different ways by early European settlers, providing food for human consumption and for domesticated animals, timber and tannin. *Justin Vance.*

Below: Harpers Ferry, located in Jefferson County, is the easternmost town in West Virginia and where Maryland, Virginia and West Virginia meet. *Carol Highsmith Collection, Library of Congress.*

Military veteran and Grafton native Tim Poling is a member of the West Virginia Department of Agriculture Veterans and Warriors to Agriculture program and is raising bees, which has helped him deal with his post-military anxiety and depression. *West Virginia Department of Agriculture.*

Pasture-raised pigs get a large part of their feed by foraging, and animals raised outside confinement are far healthier than confinement-raised pigs. Many people believe they also taste better. *Jason Nerenberg.*

Clearly, converting grain crops to whiskey was a prudent economic decision for settlers, since liquor was less bulky than the grain it was made from and more easily transported over primitive roads. But as the saying goes, nothing is certain but death and taxes, and the latter was becoming a reality for the do-it-yourself distillers of western Virginia, one that would lead to armed conflict with the fledgling government of the United States that came to be known as the Whiskey Rebellion.

Lasting from 1791 to 1794, the Whiskey Rebellion was an American frontier revolt against a federal excise tax levied on distilled spirits. The tax was created by Alexander Hamilton to pay off the remaining Revolutionary debt.

According to historian Dr. Barbara Rasmussen:

> *The rebellion also pointed out ideological and moral differences among Americans. Eastern elites saw no wrong in taxing liquor, but frontiersmen considered it a harsh economic blow to them, converting grain crops to whiskey was a prudent economic decision, since whiskey was less bulky than the grain it was made from and more easily transported over primitive roads. The rebellion contributed to the development of a hurtful stereotype, that of the violent hillbilly moonshiner. Prior to the tax, the spirits distilled in the mountains—especially Monongahela Rye (which was actually distilled from two grains—rye and barley) from the area around Morgantown including southwestern Pennsylvania—was a highly prized commodity that could fetch a top price. Merchants as far away as New Orleans were anxious to acquire it. This demand gave the farmers a cash crop.*

Despite modest advances in industry and transportation, western Virginia remained first and foremost an agrarian culture, albeit one that had evolved and improved from the hardscrabble days when the pioneers scratched out an existence under extremely trying conditions. One way to gain insight into just what life (and food) was like for early West Virginia farmers is to study what they left behind when they died. For example, the estate settlement of one Nicholas Woolf of Randolph County reveals a surprising amount of detail about what his life must have been like, what he grew, what tools he used and how his food might have been prepared:

> *According to an appraisal, Mr. Woolf possessed, in addition to his 245¼ acre landholding, several sows, pigs, steers, heifers and a mare. His farming implements included hoes, axes, sickles, and "plow irons." In spite of the*

oft-mentioned travel impediments and lack of access to goods, he had what would appear to be significant cookware: a Dutch oven, a pair of pothooks, one pewter plate and six dishes, six tin cups, a pewter "basin," twelve earthen plates, forks, spoons, knives, a tea canister, a pepper box, a butter churn and a coffee mill. In the fields he had standing crops of wheat, rye, oats and, of course, corn. All of this in addition to a spinning wheel, furniture, a great number of tools for carpentry, field work, and other tasks, and even a copy of an "English Almanac."

Although he died in 1800 and not far from the geographic center of what is now West Virginia, clearly Woolf had moved well beyond the days of cooking over an open fire under the stars. As Woolf's estate settlement illustrates, cast-iron cooking pots and pans remained the standards of food preparation and would through the nineteenth century and beyond. Even today, cast iron is popular in West Virginia.

In Ruth Woods Dayton's *Pioneers and Their Homes on Upper Kanawha* (1947) are gathered some journal entries of a Mr. Lewis Summers of Alexandria, Virginia, made while visiting the Kanawha Valley in 1808. Some of his notes are predictable, as when he mentions the loss of livestock to bears and wolves. Others are a little more surprising, such as "good cotton grown along the river." And then there is the amusing, as when he describes a Fourth of July celebration "where there was much food, dancing and 'handsome' ladies—some of the fair ones coming from as far away as Teays Valley."

While some settlers managed to establish successful farms and businesses and put down roots that would take hold, there were many others who were less successful, owing to title issues with their claims. Even early in the nineteenth century, as noted elsewhere, people coming westward would use tomahawk rights to claim title to a tract of land. They would deaden a few trees at the beginning of a spring and then mark their initials in the bark of the trees. Between 1800 and 1830, there was a lot of squatting and subsequent disputes that often complicated a clear chain of title, sometimes causing longtime residents to lose their land, and the resultant losses, litigation and uncertainty forced many families to migrate out of western Virginia farther west. By 1830, nearly half of the population had left the region.

For those who remained, the work never ceased as they developed their farms and holdings. Amid all that effort, there emerged a variety of vegetables, often unique to specific areas, the result of happy cross-pollinating accidents or deliberate experimentation by farmers and gardeners or perhaps a mixture of both. Many of these are now forgotten or nearly so, but a recent renewed interested in "heirloom vegetables" and a growing resistance to industrial farming has jump-started interest in growing varieties that have been missing from West Virginia tables for decades or even longer. In an interview in *Goldenseal* magazine in the early 1980s, writer Gerry Milnes discussed some of the heirloom beans and other plants that Braxton County resident Ruby Morris collected and grew, and her knowledge and insights provide a fascinating look into West Virginia's agricultural and culinary past. It's difficult to say what many of these tasted like, but the names are delightful. Among the beans she collected were the trout bean, white corn bean, white ice bean, lazy wife pole bean, mutton bean and purple Valentine bean. Morris's eclectic collection of heirloom vegetables did not end with beans—although at that time she was planting up to thirty varieties. She referenced a family known as the Cliftons from "up on Crites Mountain." Apparently, a number of plants the Clifton family grew, dating back to the early nineteenth century, were quite impressive, including a yellow tomato called the "Clifton Pink Beefsteak." She had great success with the "Blue River Squash" and bemoaned the loss of what was once a local favorite: the green mountain potato.

Not every experiment with a crop would prove successful. For example, around 1858, sorghum or cane was introduced to the central area of the state. In John Davison Sutton's book *A History of Braxton County and Central West Virginia*, he explains that "the people had little or no knowledge of the method of extracting the juice from the stalks, and little faith in its value as a food product."

Cabbage, in general, remained a staple crop among western Virginia farmers, and little wonder, although no significant named varieties appear to have been developed here. The popularity of the vegetable is easy to understand. All one had to do to safely store one's cabbage crop through the winter was bury it in a mound of dirt and straw, along with potatoes, and simply dig in and retrieve as needed, or they could salt and ferment it to make sauerkraut.

In 2010, the Appalachian Lifestyles blog published a list of tomatoes developed and grown in the region that included "1884, Big Sandy, Cornish, Dr. Suds Capon Bridge, Homer Fike's Yellow Oxheart, Irish Pink, Mortgage Lifter, Old German, Paw Paw, Striped German, Tappy's Finest, Toensfeldt, Transparent, Watermelon Pink and Yellow Cookie."

The tradition of making sauerkraut was brought to West Virginia by early German settlers better known as the "Pennsylvania Dutch." *Library of Congress.*

Tomato catsup recipe from 1835. *Harrison County Historical Society.*

West Virginia is home to many heirloom vegetable and fruit varieties, including the "West Virginia 63," developed by Mannon Gallegly to commemorate the state's centennial. *West Virginia Farmers Market Association.*

Perhaps the most iconic of the heirloom vegetables to emerge from the Mountain State is the provocatively named bloody butcher corn. Baker Creek Seed Company, a purveyor of heirloom varietals, describes the corn thusly:

> *A very beautiful, commonly crimson red dent variety introduced to the settlers in the Virginia area in the 1840s. Eight to twelve-foot tall stalks produce large, heavy, 8 to 12-inch long ears of solid red kernels that vary in hue. Occasional red and white kernels and ears may appear, but this is typical. It is known for its delicious, rich, sweet flavor when ground into meal and flour.*

In 2014, NPR ran a piece on the return of bloody butcher and interviewed "Edgar Meadows, 93…one saver of seeds of the corn that have been in his family for at least five generations in West Virginia. The name Bloody Butcher refers to the flecks of red mixed onto the white kernels—like a butcher's apron, Meadows says."

In Glenn Lough's *Now and Long Ago* is reprinted an unattributed brief memoir of life in Middletown (now Fairmont) in the 1820s that goes into some culinary and other detail:

> *Sometimes mother would make white biscuits using for shortening lard that she had flavored with bay leaves and other herbs. She didn't roll out or cut the dough for these biscuits, but formed them with her own dear hands, and pricked them with a fork to keep them from blistering….And with butter and jam, received from the neighbors for chores well done by us children, spread thickly on those biscuits….Who could have asked for better eating?*

The author also elaborates on the addition of fish to the household diet: "One kind of food there we had in plenty was fish. I think my brothers and I must have caught a hundred pounds of them during our first year in Middletown. We speared and netted them and sledged them through the ice. The Monongahela was teeming with fine fish in those days."

The writer mentions wolf depredations on livestock and subsequent community reaction and the construction and furnishings of the family home. But perhaps the most poignant information comes in some of the closing lines, written from a distance of many decades:

> *I can shut my eyes at any time and see in my mind our poor little cabin standing there on that hill of stones and stumps, looking down on the river,*

and my dear mother sitting on the front stoop shelling peas or stringing beans....Living in Middletown...was hard most of the time, but it made a good healthful people of all of us. I guess it was at Middletown that our family became what is spoken of today as American pioneers.

In *History of Braxton County and Central West Virginia*, Sutton pays tribute to the strength and self-reliance of the women settlers by example, noting among others a Mrs. Huffman who, when her husband neglected to kill and butcher a hog per her request, "proceeded to kill the hog herself." When her husband rose the next morning, "he found the hog hanging up neatly dressed and ready to be salted down. The hog netted two hundred pounds." "Aunt Matty" was another subject of Sutton's chronicles. It was said of her, "She was an expert hand in fruiting butters and providing sustenance for her family. She could lift a kettle of boiling apple butter off from the fire with one hand."

Whatever growth was occurring in western Virginia still tended to be fragmented. Each of the regions certainly had overlapping characteristics, but simultaneously, they evolved into distinct cultures, and those distinctions would become even more pronounced as the nineteenth century progressed. Take, for instance, the northern panhandle, which as noted stretches farther north than Pittsburgh. Hancock County is the northernmost county in West Virginia, located at the tip of the northern panhandle, and was formed in 1848. The area has a very steep and rocky terrain that made farming difficult. However, its proximity to the economic powerhouse that was the Ohio River enabled it to have commercial opportunities like fruit growing and whiskey making. In the early 1800s, the people who lived there shipped their products, especially fruit, down the Ohio to New Orleans. It was also an area with a tradition of beekeeping and maple syrup production. That steep terrain that made farming so difficult turned out to be ideal for raising sheep.

Even if there had been better access to markets, the natural resources that have driven so much of West Virginia's economic history—coal and natural gas—were not yet in demand or being used in any meaningful way anywhere in the country.

Certainly, at that time, the Monongahela River represented transport to Pittsburgh and points beyond the frontier and the potential for much more in the future if its flows could be stabilized. Ironically, the Ohio River was something of a "super-highway" for many people heading west to settle, and as such, there was some opportunity for the sale of goods and services in settlements and towns that lined its shores along the western border of the state. But the vast interior could contribute little to that avenue of commerce and benefited even less. The major markets for goods remained back east, over the mountains, and it would not be until the development of dependable roads and rails that larger-scale, urban development became possible for many parts of the region. The slow pace of infrastructure development persisted until after the Civil War and the rise of the extractive industries in the form of timbering and coal mining.

That is not to say there was no development. Road systems slowly but surely evolved out of footpaths, both human and game, and wagon trails. Routes were established between important communities, towns and cities, such as the Staunton-Parkersburg Turnpike or the Beverly Pike, which traveled between the current site of Fairmont and the community of Beverly in Randolph. Today, the latter is better known as part of Route 250.

The Northwestern Turnpike was established by charter in 1827 and was the forerunner of the modern Route 50. The road was mapped out to run from Winchester, Virginia, through Romney, Grafton and Clarksburg to its terminus on the Ohio River at Parkersburg, stretching nearly 240 miles. According to Sutton's *History of Braxton County and Central West Virginia*, "Wagons hauling 4000 pounds of goods were about fifteen days on the road from Baltimore," and at Parkersburg, steamboat connections could be made.

Perhaps the most famous of the early transportation projects to pass through the Mountain State is the National Road (today's Route 40). While it may be hard to believe, the National Road was for many years also something of a super-highway that represented a determined effort to create a dependable route from the East into the Midwest that would serve migrating settlers as well as purveyors of business. The road started in Cumberland, Maryland, in 1811, following the famed Braddock's Road from the French and Indian War era, reaching Wheeling in 1818. In 1849, work on a suspension bridge to allow the National Road to cross the Ohio River at Wheeling was completed. The road only passes through West Virginia's northern panhandle for a short distance, but it nonetheless made a great impact, particularly on the growing city of Wheeling. Inns, taverns and stagecoach stations lined the road, and the flow of traffic brought prosperity to communities that lined its path, as well as something of a culture of its own. The importance of the road continued well into the twentieth century and only declined with the rise of the interstate highway system.

In his work *The Potomac*, author Frederick Gutheim offers up a vision of life on the National Road, quoting young engineering officer John Pickell, who in 1835 observed that the road was "literally covered with horsemen, wagons, and other vehicles, forming an unbroken line...to the far west. Thousands of immigrants, almost daily were seen."

Every mile between Wheeling and Cumberland was marked with a milepost. Gutheim also quotes a veteran wagoner who reminisced on nights in the taverns:

> *After supper the waggoneers would gather in the bar rooms and listen to the music of the violin furnished by one of their fellows, have a "Virginia hoe-down," sing songs, tell anecdotes...and when it was all over, lay them down on the floor before the bar room fire, side-by-side and sleep, with their feet to the fire.*

Eastbound traffic on the road would include "bacon and hams, whisky... Ohio tobacco, lard, cheese, flour, corn, oats, and other farm produce. Westbound traffic...included paint, hardware, merchandise, and the great winter traffic in oysters." The aforementioned wagoner also recollected a stay in adjoining Maryland, whereupon he witnessed "thirty-six horse teams in the wagon yard, one hundred Kentucky mares on an adjacent lot, one thousand hogs in other enclosures, and as many fat cattle from Illinois in adjoining field."

Development was not limited to overland travel. West Virginia's interior may have presented little opportunity for commercial navigation, but the same was not true for the Ohio and Potomac border watersheds, although for two different reasons.

The Potomac long inspired forward-thinking individuals like George Washington to develop a way to ship goods and passengers from the frontier to the Chesapeake Bay and beyond. Plans were promoted to develop a canal system to parallel the river, utilizing towpaths, locks, dams and even tunnels, to make water travel possible as far upriver as Cumberland, Maryland, which sits across the river from what is now West Virginia. The resultant Chesapeake & Ohio (C&O) Canal served for decades, moving cargo up and down from Alexandria, and with a unique culture of its own, though ultimately it never achieved the success its founders had hoped for. By the time it was operational, the railroads were coming—and they would soon dwarf the competition.

It was also on the Potomac near Shepherdstown, in 1787, that inventor James Rumsey designed and built a steamboat, contributing mightily to the efforts of many to develop reliable machine-driven water travel. It would

This R.R. Hudson steamboat was built in 1866. Until railroads reached West Virginia, steamboats were the major mode of mass transportation of people and goods. *Library of Congress.*

be on the Ohio River, however, that the steamboat would have the greatest impact on the Mountain State. The ability to travel upstream against the current meant that not only could people and material be sent into the Midwest and Deep South but raw materials could be brought back. As early as 1811, a primitive steam-powered vessel traveled from Pittsburgh all the way to New Orleans, passing along its way the fledgling communities of Wheeling, Parkersburg, Point Pleasant and others. Wheeling, in fact, was for a time the site of steamboat construction. The flatboats and keel boats—both iconic contributors to early river traffic during the westward expansion—hung on for decades, but mechanized boats were here to stay and dominate.

In the eastern panhandle, life continued to resemble that of Northern Virginia and Maryland mixed with a heavy German influence. In his landmark study of the iconic river, *The Potomac*, Frederick Gutheim painted a picture of the farmers of German descent who had done much to develop farming in the eastern panhandle:

> *The fortified stone houses and log houses and big barns of the Pennsylvania Germans were to be found up and down...the Shenandoah and South*

Branch....Their red cattle and fields of corn and wheat fit easily into the Piedmont landscape. Their industry, their arts, their songs still give the region its unmistakable flavor and originality.

As for a validating example of the Virginia-Maryland influence on the region, we can look, interestingly, at the writing of a man at least partially responsible for escalating the looming Civil War. John Brown took time to paint a picture of what life was like on a farm that, though in Maryland, would absolutely resemble those across the Potomac in the eastern panhandle in the 1850s. In Osborne P. Anderson's *A Voice from Harper's Ferry: A Narrative of Events at Harper's Ferry; with Incidents Prior and Subsequent to Its Capture by Captain Brown and His Men,* the infamous abolitionist mentions pawpaws while at his home on Kennedy Farm:

We were, while the ladies remained, often relieved of much of the dullness growing out of restraint by their kindness. As we could not circulate freely, they would bring in wild fruit and flowers from the woods and fields. We were well supplied with grapes, paw-paws, chestnuts, and other small fruit, besides bouquets of fall flowers, through their thoughtful consideration.

The Kennedy Farm is an American landmark where John Brown planned and began his raid on Harpers Ferry, West Virginia, in 1859. Brown was captured, tried and hanged for his actions. His actions contributed to slaves being freed in 1865, six years after his death.

The meal a traveler might encounter in Shepherdstown or Martinsburg would differ vastly from the meager fare offered up at a tavern in one of the sparsely settled mountain counties. As ever, despite whatever successes and progress they may enjoy from year to year, the fate of farmers rested with the weather. In a letter dated March 27, 1842, Harrison County farmer Elisha Hall noted, "Our crops of wheat are about common; but it is very dry now; if we don't get rain soon there will be light crops of corn this season. Money is very scarce and no sale of stock of any sort."

Well into the nineteenth century, particularly prior to the rise of large-scale timbering operations, the region was already attracting recreational visitors to its more remote regions in a precursor to what would ultimately become a cornerstone of West Virginia's modern-day economy: tourism. More specifically, tourism that attracted outdoor sports enthusiasts. One such excursion resulted in a book and accompanying illustrations that became a milestone in outdoor sports literature and captured the remote, rugged beauty of West Virginia's thinly settled interior. Berkeley County native David Hunter Strother was a writer and artist (among other pursuits) who rose to popularity under the pseudonym Porte Crayon. He accompanied his cousin Philip Pendleton Kennedy and some other friends into the nearly impenetrable laurel thickets that encircled Blackwater Falls and Canaan Valley, in present-day Tucker County, to do some fishing and camping. The subsequent book, *The Blackwater Chronicles*, written by Kennedy and illustrated by Crayon, was published in 1853 to much success. As the *West Virginia Encyclopedia* notes, "Kennedy provides modern readers with a glimpse of a portion of present West Virginia that was then untouched by agriculture or industry. The classic book is regarded today as an important ecological document, as well as fine local color writing." Kennedy's witty writing, while definitely of another era, nonetheless paints a vivid picture of the wilds of the Blackwater country—and that includes dining. "While preparations for supper were going on, several of the party got out their fishing tackle, and tried the little stream that watered the glade. It was alive with trout; and half an hour later, a hundred of the small fry were served up with biscuit and bacon."

When they finally encounter the magnificent Blackwater Falls, Kennedy's humor contrasts delightfully with the scene, simultaneously injecting some humanization and relatability to the explorers, one of whom remarks about the torrent of water spilling over the falls that "I wish to heaven it was beer; I could drink a barrel of it on the spot."

In the 1850s, the railroad began to penetrate the interior of western Virginia and brought some level of economic diversification with it, although the major benefits of rail travel and transport would not be realized until the development of the coal and timber industries after the Civil War. Certainly, the advent of the railroad transformed once-sleepy agricultural villages like Fairmont into larger towns with expanded infrastructure in the form of bridges, telegraph lines, hotels and the like.

Nationally, the rise of the railroad, in hindsight, occurred incredibly quickly. As described in a publication by Washington, D.C.'s Southwest Neighborhood Assembly:

Between 1825 and 1915, the United States went from having zero miles of railroad track to having 254,000 miles, as much as the rest of the world combined. Railroads tied together a national transport web of rivers, canals, roads, and coastal waters. They also provided a far faster and cheaper method of transporting every imaginable kind of product, from cast iron stoves to crates of oranges and kegs of beer.

Partnered with advances in refrigeration, canning and packaging, the railroad would revolutionize life—and eating—in the United States. It was in effect the beginning of the industrialization of food—and the decline of many farm holdings in the East. Railroads run where needed, however, and development logically confined itself to the tracks and not far beyond, so much of the region remained isolated and populated by subsistence farms and homesteads. Even with the construction of the railroad, western Virginia seemed no closer to Richmond—particularly as the railroad, the Baltimore & Ohio, originated in Maryland.

The relative isolation and a tendency to stay put created strong ties to family, land and community, and with the rise of income inequality between farmers and the land-rich elite, great numbers of the former remained subsistence farmers for decades. Throughout the late eighteenth century and well into the nineteenth, the general isolation and lack of industry resulted in western Virginia's chief form of economic activity being the barter system. All these conditions led to difficulties with banking and political representation. Regarding banking, simply put, in many areas there were often no banks and no ready cash to deposit in a bank were it to be established. As for the latter, Richmond, the center of state government, was hundreds of miles away. This is not to say the residents across the mountains were completely powerless. For example, Clarksburg resident Joseph Johnson was elected governor a decade before the Civil War. But in general, the very real obstacles and space between the two populations (not to mention their widening cultural gap) strained the relationship between the two regions. This is readily apparent when one considers the upper panhandle region alone stretches farther north than Pittsburgh. It's not difficult to see how disagreements could—and did—arise. By and large, Virginia proper and western Virginia were developing into two distinctly different entities. By 1861, at the beginning of the Civil War, western Virginia's population was a little over 420,000 people compared to a population of over 1,170,000 people in the counties that make up modern-day Virginia. The chain of mountains that separated the two regions was probably the single biggest reason for the disconnect between the peoples of the two regions, although certainly not the only one. There was also the matter of slavery.

The slave population in what is now West Virginia remained tiny in comparison to that of Virginia proper, even as the general slave population in the mother state declined. This resulted in a political imbalance as eastern Virginia used that larger slave population to secure political power that would reward that region disproportionately in a variety of areas, including education and infrastructure. Given the magnitude of differences between eastern and western Virginia, it seems logical that at some point a breach between the two would have occurred regardless of whether civil war broke out. But break out it did, making West Virginia's statehood not only a possibility but a reality.

Virginia voted to secede from the Union in April 1861. In May, a convention of delegates selected from the western counties met in Wheeling to determine whether western Virginia should stay in the Union or secede with Virginia to the Confederacy. They voted on May 23, 1861, against secession, choosing to remain loyal to the Union. July 18, 1861, marked the beginning of the Second Wheeling Convention, which led to the creation of the Reorganized Government of Virginia. Thus, Virginia had two state governments throughout the war: one in Richmond, under the Confederacy, and one in Wheeling, loyal to the United States. Several Marion County natives were critical to this effort, including Waitman T. Willey, who went on to become a United States senator, and Francis Harrison Pierpont, who was elected governor of Restored Virginia. By May 1862, the United States Congress was presented with the constitution and proposal for the new state of West Virginia. The Senate passed the bill admitting West Virginia on July 14, 1862, and the House of Representatives did likewise on December 10, 1862.

Most of western Virginia was Union, but there was nonetheless a substantial number of Confederates in the area, even in the northern counties. Take Marion County, which was the quintessential border county, wherein political differences often pitted neighbor against neighbor, family member against family member. Being home to Francis Harrison Pierpont heightened the county's importance from merely strategic to symbolic. Pierpont was extremely unpopular among the Confederates and presented a tantalizing target. That coupled with the strategically important B&O Railroad bridge across the Monongahela led the county, and Fairmont in particular, into the sights of Confederate general William E. "Grumble" Jones. The Jones-Imboden Raid brought the violence and destruction of the war right to the doorsteps of the residents of north-central West Virginia.

Much of western Virginia's soil was spared from the larger, bloodier battles of the Civil War, although ironically it was home to the first land skirmish of the conflict, which was fought in Philippi. However, both before and

One of the most popular ways to serve ramps is with fried potatoes, eggs, sausage and bacon. An acquired taste for some, the ramp was nonetheless highly sought after by early settlers craving the first greens of the season. *Author's collection.*

after statehood, and for the entirety of the war, the region remained a hotly contested border, which meant continual strife. Many crops and animals were destroyed during the war, having a huge impact on agricultural life and trade. At times, people lived on what could be found or foraged in the forests, like venison. Anxiety about food and crops ran high in peacetime due to the weather and precipitation. The constant threat of predation, violence, looting and scavenging only exacerbated that anxiety. When soldier Joseph Tinnel of Nicholas County, who served in the Confederacy, wrote home to his wife in 1862, he was careful to advise her on farm matters, including "to sell any property or anything that you have on the place if necessity requires. If I should not return before corn planting I want you [to] have some corn planted in the best of ground where we had corn year before last you will have to do the best you can and hire someone to do your spring work if I am not there in time to do it myself."

As fate would have it, Tinnel would not return home that spring or ever; he was one of the over 600,000 Americans who perished in the war.

❖ ❖ ❖

West Virginia Ramp Breakfast

1 pound bacon or sausage or both
1 cup ramps, white parts and leaves, chopped coarsely
5 medium-size potatoes, peeled and slivered
1 dozen large eggs
½ cup milk or cream
Salt and pepper to taste

Cook bacon or sausage in a large frying pan; remove, drain and set aside. Using the same pan with the reserved bacon fat, fry ramps and potatoes over low heat, covered, until potatoes are tender and browned. Set aside on a plate. Whisk the eggs, milk and salt and pepper together and scramble the eggs. Enjoy!

❖ ❖ ❖

Pickled Eggs and Ramps

6 eggs
1 cup wild ramp whites
1 ½ cups apple cider vinegar
1 ½ cups water
2 tablespoons pickling salt
1 tablespoon whole black peppercorns
1 tablespoon whole red peppercorns
1 tablespoon red pepper flakes
2 sprigs rosemary

Cover the eggs with cold water and bring to a boil. Turn heat off and cover with a lid. Peel eggs when cooled. Wash the ramps and trim the green leaves off. In a large metal saucepan, bring vinegar to a boil with water, pickling salt, black peppercorns, red peppercorns and red pepper flakes. Place peeled eggs into a clean wide-mouth quart glass jar and layer in the wild ramp whites and two sprigs of rosemary. Fill jar with pickling brine and seal jar tightly. Place jar in the refrigerator and let rest for 3 days. Eat the pickled eggs within another 3 days.

❖ ❖ ❖

West Virginia Soup Beans

1 (16-ounce) package dried pinto beans
1 large onion, diced
3 stalks celery
3 carrots
1 teaspoon butter or bacon grease
1 meaty hambone or ham hocks
2 quarts water
Salt and pepper to taste
Pinch of hot pepper flakes

Place beans in a large pot covered with water and soak overnight. Drain water off beans. Chop the onions, celery and carrots together in a food processor. In a large pot, sauté the onion, carrots and celery in fat. Add the beans and water, throw in the ham bone and cook on medium heat. Once the beans begin to lightly boil at medium heat, lower the temperature to low, cover and cook for about 2 hours. Every half hour or so, uncover beans and give them a stir, making sure they are simmering in enough cooking liquid. If beans appear dry, add a little more water. Once beans are tender, season with salt and pepper to taste and a pinch of red pepper flakes. If you salt them too early, they can be tough and cook unevenly.

❖ ❖ ❖

Cornbread

1 tablespoon bacon fat or butter
1 cup all-purpose flour

1 cup yellow cornmeal
1 teaspoon sugar
3 teaspoons baking powder
¼ teaspoon baking soda
½ teaspoon salt
3 tablespoons melted shortening or butter
1 cup milk
2 eggs, beaten

Preheat oven to 425 degrees. Place 1 tablespoon of bacon fat or butter in a 10-inch cast-iron skillet and place on the center rack of the oven. Combine the flour, cornmeal, sugar, baking powder, baking soda and salt in a bowl. Mix until well blended. Add the shortening, milk and eggs. Do not overmix. Remove the preheated skillet from the oven and turn the skillet so the sides of the skillet are coated in oil. Pour batter into skillet and bake for 25 to 30 minutes.

How to season your cast-iron skillet:
Scrub with soapy water. Then scour with coarse salt. This will get any of the dried food bits and dullness off. Rinse and dry well; do not let the skillet air dry, as this will lead to rust. Rub the skillet with vegetable oil using a paper towel. Place skillet upside down in a 350-degree oven and bake for 1 hour. Let skillet cool in oven.

❖ ❖ ❖

Sausage Gravy and Biscuits

1 pound ground sausage
5 tablespoons all-purpose flour
3 tablespoons butter
4 cups milk
Salt and pepper to taste

Brown sausage in large saucepan; strain most grease after browning sausage. Sprinkle the flour over sausage and cook for a few minutes so the flour doesn't taste raw. Cover the sausage with milk. Place on medium heat and stir constantly until the mix begins to thicken. Add salt and pepper to taste.

❖ ❖ ❖

Biscuits

2 cups sifted flour
½ teaspoon salt
½ teaspoon baking soda
4 tablespoons Crisco shortening
¾ cup buttermilk

Sift the flour. In a bowl or on the counter, add flour, salt and baking soda. Cut in the shortening with a fork. Make a well in the center of the mixture and add the buttermilk and mix well. Turn dough onto a floured counter. The dough should be stiff and soft but not sticky. Lightly knead the dough a few times and roll out to about ½-inch thickness. Cut with a floured cutter or mason jar. Place on an ungreased baking sheet. Bake in 425-degree oven until golden brown, about 12 to 15 minutes.

❖ ❖ ❖

Preston County Buckwheat Cakes

This recipe was found in an old collection of recipes, and no date appears. It was approved by Miss Roxie King, who mixed batter and baked cakes at every Preston County Buckwheat Festival. Miss Roxie is fondly called Miss Buckwheat.

1 quart lukewarm water
¼ cake large household yeast, thicken to stiff batter with 2½ cups of Buckwheat Flour and ½ cup of wheat flour

Cover and let rise overnight.

The next morning, dissolve 1 teaspoon of baking soda, 2 teaspoons of sugar in ½ cup of milk and enough warm water to make batter thin enough to bake. Bake what is needed to serve, and place rest in the refrigerator as a starter.

To renew at night (or at least three or four hours before use), add 1 cup lukewarm water to starter, 1 cup buckwheat flour, ¼ cup of wheat flour. When ready to serve, do as above: dissolve 1 teaspoon of baking soda, 2 teaspoons of sugar in ½ cup of milk and enough water to make a thin batter. Bake or griddle what is needed.

One does not need to use more yeast for several mornings, then use as Miss Roxie will tell you, only a "pinch" (about ¼ teaspoon).

❖ ❖ ❖

Deer Steak and Onion Gravy

2 pounds deer steak
1 cup vinegar
1 tablespoon salt
Salt and pepper to taste
Flour for dredging steak
1 tablespoon bacon grease or butter
1 large onion
3 cloves minced garlic
5 tablespoons flour
½ cup milk or half-and-half
1 cup beef stock

Soak deer steak in vinegar, salt and enough water to cover overnight in refrigerator. Drain well. Pat dry. Season with salt and pepper. Dredge in flour. Place in hot skillet with grease and brown on each side. Remove from pan.

Meanwhile, in the skillet, add the chopped onion to the deer drippings. Cook on medium-low heat until the onion starts to soften and brown. Add garlic and cook until soft. Add the remaining butter and flour to the pan. Cook the flour a few minutes until it darkens. Add the milk and beef stock. Cook on medium heat, continually stirring with a whisk, for about

5 minutes. Place the deer steaks in pan and cover with the gravy. Cover with foil and bake in a preheated 350-degree oven for 30 minutes. Serve with mashed potatoes, buttered noodles or rice.

❖ ❖ ❖

Green Beans

2 pounds green beans
1 ham hock
2 teaspoons salt
Pinch of hot pepper flakes

Wash the beans, cut off ends and snap in two. In a large kettle, place the beans, ham hock, salt and pepper flakes and cover with water. Cook for an hour.

❖ ❖ ❖

Chicken and Dumplings

Large fryer chicken (4–5 pounds), neck and gizzards removed
1 large onion, chopped
3 carrots, chopped
3 stalks celery, chopped
3 cloves garlic, minced
1 bunch fresh parsley, chopped
Salt and pepper to taste

Dumplings
3 cups flour
¾ teaspoon baking soda
¾ teaspoon salt
3 tablespoons shortening
1 cup milk

Chicken and
dumplings.
*Author's
collection.*

Place the chicken in a large pot and cover with water. Bring to a boil, then reduce heat so water maintains a gentle simmer. Cook chicken for 1 hour. Once chicken is done, remove from the broth and let cool. Remove chicken from the bone (this shouldn't be hard; it should be falling off easily at this point) and shred into medium-sized pieces, discarding bones and skin. Add the chopped onions, carrots, celery and garlic to the simmering stock and cook for about 20 minutes. Add the chicken back to the stock with the chopped parsley.

To make the dumplings, mix flour, baking soda and salt in a bowl. Cut shortening into flour mixture with your fingertips until it resembles small peas. Add milk—¼ cup at a time, you may not need a full cup— and stir until a ball of dough just begins to form, being careful not to over-mix. Roll out the dough onto floured surface about ¼ inch thick. Using a pizza cutter or sharp knife, cut dough into rectangles about 1 inch wide by 3 inches long. Add the dumplings to the simmering broth, cover and allow to cook for 10 to 15 minutes, then reduce heat to low and let cook for about 20 to 30 minutes.

❖ ❖ ❖

Bonnie Jean's Applesauce Cake

2½ cups flour
2 cups sugar
1½ teaspoons baking soda
1½ teaspoons salt
¼ teaspoon baking powder
¾ teaspoon cinnamon
½ teaspoon cloves
½ teaspoon allspice
1½ cups applesauce
½ cup water
½ cup shortening
2 eggs
1 cup raisins

Heat oven to 350 degrees. Grease and flour a baking or Bundt pan. Measure all ingredients in a large mixing bowl. Beat for 30 seconds on low speed then 3 minutes on high speed, occasionally scraping the bowl. Pour into a pan. Bake for an hour or until a toothpick inserted in the center comes out clean.

❖ ❖ ❖

Pan-Fried Trout

8 to 10 trout fillets
2 cups bread crumbs
1 teaspoon salt
½ teaspoon garlic powder
½ teaspoon paprika
1 teaspoon cornstarch
2 tablespoons beer
1 egg
Vegetable oil for frying

Rinse fillets and pat dry. Blend bread crumbs and spices together. Whisk together the cornstarch and beer, then add the egg and whisk again. Place the fillets in the egg mixture and set aside for about 10 minutes.

Remove the fillets from the mixture and dredge in the bread crumbs, making sure the fillets are evenly coated. Heat vegetable oil in a cast-iron skillet until it is screaming hot. Immediately add the breaded fillets and cook for about 2 to 3 minutes or until the fillets brown, which should happen quickly. Turn the fillets over and cook for another 2 to 3 minutes.

Chapter 5
INDUSTRIALIZATION, IMMIGRATION AND THE TWENTIETH CENTURY

T he Industrial Revolution was gaining momentum in the years following the Civil War and it would deliver significant change at last for West Virginians in the form of industry, cultural diversity and, for some, prosperity (although often at terrible cost). The change was initially driven by improved access to transportation in the form of the railroad. The expansion of the railroad encouraged wealthy capitalists to flood into the state and take advantage of the abundance of all the natural resources: timber, natural gas, petroleum and coal. Many West Virginia farmers were leery of the railroad as they feared that the destruction of property and livestock would cause economic losses. They also knew the railroad would bring in cheaper goods, which they could not compete with. But some farmers who lived near the railroads saw it as an opportunity to sell more goods and make more money.

The Grange, a farmers' association, formed nationally in 1867 and in 1873 came to West Virginia with the goal of providing farmers with the most up-to-date agricultural information to lobby against high railroad transportation costs and high tariffs on imported goods and also for rural mail delivery. It gave rural, isolated farmers and their families a place to socialize. Nonetheless, by the end of the nineteenth century, there began a decline in West Virginia farms. People began leaving farms and moving to towns or cities for industrial work. Farming was usually a family affair with tasks split between family members, and now that way of life was threatened, and not just because of the exodus of farmers and their kin.

In an 1887 letter from Thomas Sturm to his brother John Sturm, he talks about concerns for his crops: "We had a very dry summer and fall in our country. Corn is very lite, wheat prity good and oats good for the season and drought hit wheat worth 100." In the best of times, there was harvest insecurity for farmers. In addition to the normal issues, like weather, there were new threats to the agrarian way of life. The impact of large-scale extraction operations like logging and mining was drastically transforming the lands and waters of West Virginia. This combined with the movement away from the family farm would dramatically alter farming, hunting, fishing and foraging, which would in turn affect the state's foodways.

The expansion of manufacturing, transportation, mining and communication created unprecedented wealth for many, especially the absentee landowners who purchased large tracts of land for the exploitation of natural resources. This would become an ongoing theme in West Virginia and a major factor in the development of the state, including the way West Virginians prepared, processed, preserved and ate their food.

As late as 1880, over two-thirds of West Virginia was covered by old-growth forests, which were suddenly quite attractive to titans of industry, particularly given their proximity to the East Coast's exploding industrial activity. Logging operations were jump-started, with the construction of work camps and access roads and even short-line railroads. Men were recruited to work as lumberjacks, sawmill operators and general laborers and support staff.

Life in the camps was rough. Men got up before dawn and worked until dark. But their pay was fair, and the food is reported to have been great. Lore states that workers would leave one camp for another if it had a better cook. These men burned thousands of calories a day, so food was a big motivator and very important to them. They ate bacon, eggs, ham, toast and coffee for breakfast; multiple sandwiches for lunch; and meat, potatoes, vegetables and biscuits for dinner.

For all the visual and environmental impact timbering would have on the mountains and waters of West Virginia, its influence pales in comparison to the industrial-scale extractive practice that would come to dominate the state's economy, culture and image: coal mining.

West Virginia's coal mining history dates to the late eighteenth century, when the area was still part of Virginia. Residents at the time were known to dig up small outcrops of coal to heat their homes. With the introduction and expansion of the railroad, especially the Chesapeake & Ohio Railroad to

Huntington in 1873, which opened the southern coalfields, the coal industry exploded by the 1880s. Think about this: fifty-three of the fifty-five West Virginia counties have mineable coal and produce more than one-third of the coal in the United States.

Once it was discovered that southern coal was of a higher quality than northern coal and thus more valuable, coal prices skyrocketed, spurring more development of mines, which in turn meant that the mine owners and operators needed more workers to keep up with demand. West Virginia's population was not large enough to staff the necessary workforce. Mining companies (and eventually other industries like steel making) began recruiting immigrants from Southern and Eastern Europe and African Americans from other states to work the mines, plants and factories.

Between 1820 and 1919, over thirty million immigrants from northern Europe, eastern Europe, Russia, Poland, Austria, China, Greece, France, Italy, Belgium, Croatia, Syria, Lebanon and elsewhere came to the United States and places like West Virginia to escape poverty. For some, there was also the opportunity to escape political and religious persecution. Many who came had hopes of making some extra money and returning to their home countries. Great numbers of immigrants arrived at processing centers, most famously Ellis Island. Some were greeted by family members who had already come over, while others were met by hiring agents, including many who would point them to West Virginia to the coal mines, mills, glass factories and other emerging industrial operations, like Homer Laughlin China, which opened in 1907, and Weirton Steel Corporation (1909).

As mentioned earlier, most immigrants during the colonial era were northern and western Europeans who spoke English and were Protestants. During the Industrial Revolution, this changed with the arrival of southern and eastern Europeans (Italians, Greeks, Turks, Russians, Slavs, Poles and Jews) who did not speak English and held different religious views. The cultural differences and language barriers sometimes created problems and transformed local communities, reshaped politics and created a new labor force in the Mountain State.

In the first decades following the Civil War, West Virginia's African American population had fluctuated, generally declining as many were on the move to reunite with their families after being released from bondage. Leased convicts, many of them African Americans tried for petty crimes, were also brought to West Virginia to work cleaning up after the Civil War and to build the railroads. Folk legend John Henry was reputedly one of these convict laborers who came to the state. After they finished building the

Above: West Virginia's abundant natural resources fueled production of quality earthenware, pottery and glassware. This Lewis Hines photo is of two child laborers at Morgantown Glass. *Library of Congress.*

Right: Seeking jobs created by the booming Industrial Revolution, European immigrants (along with their foodways) usually arrived first at Ellis Island in New York for processing. *Library of Congress.*

railroads, many African Americans went to work in the coal mines and were instrumental in the expansion of the coal industry.

Coal companies found it more cost effective to build entire towns around the inexhaustible seams of black mountain ridge coal. These communities were called coal camps and were very much "pop-up" towns. Coal camps hearkened back to boomtowns of the Wild West; law enforcement was minimal, and residents relied on the coal companies for homes, schools, government buildings, medical treatment and even shopping in the company store. Though the workplace was generally integrated, the company town was planned to keep the aboveground community separated not only racially but also socially and economically. In keeping with the times, the only thing not segregated was the company store, where employees and their families bought food, clothing, household items, tools and other essentials. Though the workplace was generally integrated, the company town was planned to keep the aboveground community separated not only racially but also socially and economically. In keeping with the times, the only thing not segregated was the company store, where employees and their families bought food, clothing, household items, tools and other essentials. Workers were paid in company "scrip," a type of currency that was created by the coal company and could only be used at the company store. Many miners, especially the immigrant ones, were caught in a vicious cycle of trying to pay off their peonage and their company store debt.

Although these immigrants brought their foodways with them, they didn't necessarily have ready access to the ingredients their recipes required, so they improvised and used what was locally available and adapted their recipes. Ultimately, some of them would open markets that catered to the hunger

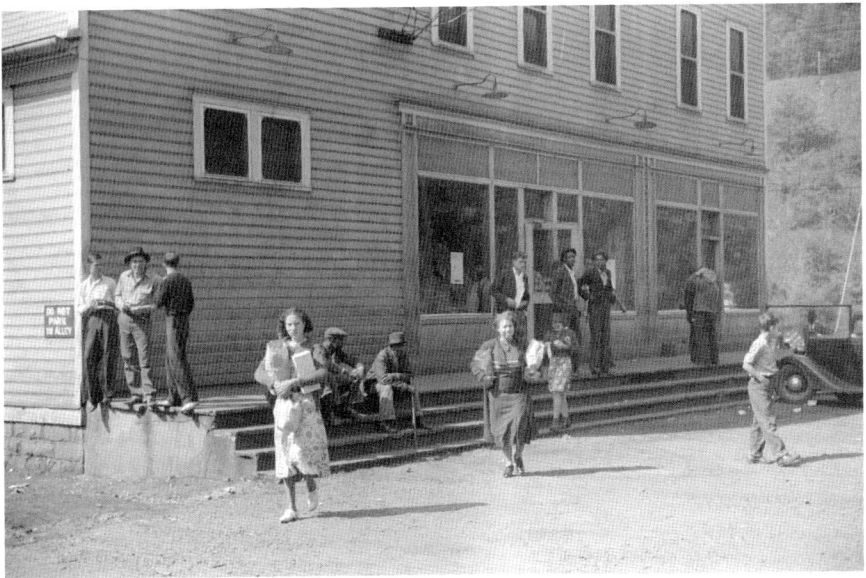

Most every coal camp/town had a company store—an establishment owned by the mining company that sold necessities to the miners and their families. *Library of Congress.*

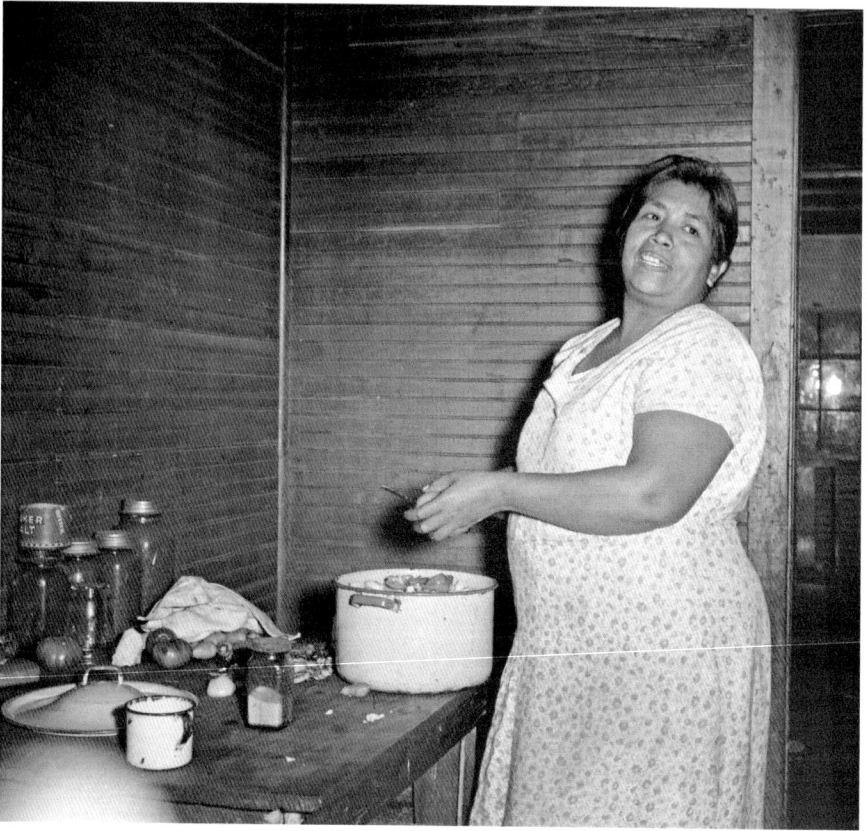

West Virginia coal camps were often ethnically diverse and home to multiple languages, religions, traditions and cuisines. This Mexican miner's wife is cooking stew. *Library of Congress.*

for the tastes of home and the comfort that would accompany practicing traditional methods of preparing dishes, observing holidays and the like.

The first generation of immigrants who lived in the coal camps often built outdoor ovens. Italian immigrants Concetta Quattrone, who arrived in McDowell County in 1918, and Cynthia Cardea Earnest joined their neighbors in making bread in round brick ovens similar to the ones they had used in Italy. The ovens were built near their houses in the coal camp at Vivian, presumably by the same European stonemasons who built the round beehive coke ovens in coal mining operations throughout southern West Virginia.

In an interview with Bonnie Oliverio Tinnell, she recalls time spent with her Italian grandmother:

Immigrants brought foodways and customs to the area and also learned to adapt those foodways to what grew locally and was available. *Library of Congress.*

My Italian grandmother Oliverio was a master gardener. She lived off her garden, and even in the winter you could step outside the kitchen door and pick some kind of green leafy vegetable for a salad. She maintained her own hot beds and kept seeds from year to year, having tomatoes from the old country. She gardened up until the time of her death and was remembered in our town for her khaki-colored army fatigue hat she wore for gardening. Her shelves were always filled with wonderful tomato sauces, canned peppers, canned mushrooms and homegrown vegetables. Potatoes were not a staple in her house, but you never stopped in that a bowl of pasta didn't appear within minutes. I loved the balls of provolone hanging in her basement and the wonderful dry bread and salty pizzas. The bread was always wrapped in a clean white cloth, and she held the loaf against her breasts as she cut off thick slices. She was a winemaker, and we loved playing around the barrels in her basement but were warned to never touch the taps.

These immigrants clung to their foodways but also had to learn to adapt, and that's just what immigrant Joseph "Giuseppe" Argiro did in 1927 when he created the pepperoni roll. The pepperoni roll is to West

Virginia what the cheesesteak is to Philadelphia or the bagel to New York City. Argiro noticed that many of the miners would fold bread around a pepperoni stick. Miners needed portable food that could be easily handled and would have a longer shelf life in case they were trapped underground. Argiro created a yeast dough, stuffed it with pepperoni and baked it. Thus, the pepperoni roll was born.

Traditionalists insist that a real pepperoni roll is a yeast dough with a stick of pepperoni baked in it and topped with butter while steaming hot. Other methods include using frozen dough or crescent dough or grinding or slicing the pepperoni. Hot dog chili, cheese, peppers and sauce—or a combination of these—are often added to pepperoni rolls. In 2013, a bill was introduced to the West Virginia House of Delegates to make the pepperoni roll the official West Virginia state food.

Around the turn of the century, farmers began experiencing the impact of bad practices, including over-farming the land, neglecting fertilizing and failing to practice crop rotations. Efforts were made to educate the next generation of farmers in the form of two clubs: 4-H and Future Farmers of America (FFA). 4-H (the *H* standing for head, hand, heart and health) began in 1911 and, among other things, encouraged children to raise animals and

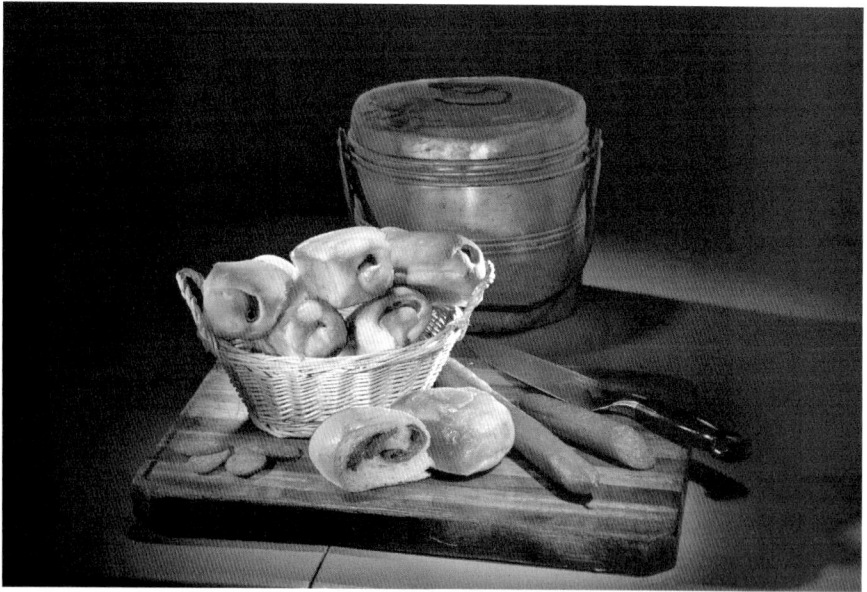

The perfect portable food miners could bring into the mines for their lunch is now the state food, albeit unofficially—pepperoni rolls. *Chuck Warner.*

crops. Similarly, the FFA also taught kids about the importance of agriculture and the business of selling goods, including a yearly auction, often at county fairs, where members sell the goods and animals they have produced and raised. West Virginia University, established in 1867, opened an Agriculture Experiment Station in 1889 that educated farmers on ways to better their farms and farming techniques.

In 1913, the West Virginia legislature passed an act to meet educational needs for farm families by hiring extension agents to go out into the field and educate farmers and their families on agricultural advancements and domestic science. During that same year, West Virginia University started offering extension schools taught by local home economic teachers.

From 1914 to 1918, World War I ravished Europe. The destruction was catastrophic, including a devastating food shortage. European farms were turned into battlefields, and the men were away fighting. The burden of feeding millions of starving people fell on the American people, and the people of West Virginia, a state with one of the highest numbers of citizens serving in the military, took the call very seriously. Over fifty-eight thousand

A woman proudly displaying canned goods. Extension services grew out of the tradition of local agricultural clubs and societies that were established throughout the country after the American Revolution. *Library of Congress.*

West Virginians served in World War I. People were encouraged to plant gardens and harvest and store their own fruits and vegetables so that the government could send more food to our allies. People also were voluntarily rationing wheat, meat, fat and sugar. Girl Scouts started to have home bake sales to raise money for war efforts. The end of the war brought no "peace dividend" to West Virginia—in fact, quite the opposite.

After the end of World War I in 1918, the demand for coal dropped drastically and so did the price, weakening the union's position. Wartime wage controls were lifted, paving the way for the operators to go back to a nonunion workforce. Soon men were being forced to sign so-called yellow dog contracts, in which they agreed to work for the company as a nonunion worker at a lower wage or risk being fired and evicted from the company-owned homes they shared with their families. Many men signed these agreements, while others stayed firm with the union and tapped their seething discontent to fuel a massive strike in which over twenty thousand miners walked off the job. Agricultural prices also declined as there was too much surplus.

West Virginia is not often in front of national trends, but the state enacted its own version of Prohibition in 1914, well before the national amendment that passed in 1919. And just as Prohibition unleashed unintended consequences on the national front, namely in the rise of organized crime courtesy of bootlegging, so did West Virginia's efforts embolden do-it-yourself distillers, who often practiced techniques handed down for generations. The moonshiner thus entered the national consciousness in such a way that the name and the practice carried on long after the repeal of Prohibition in 1933. It wasn't until almost 1990 in West Virginia that spirits could be purchased somewhere other than a state-owned liquor store.

Food security was still a constant source of anxiety for rural West Virginians, especially in mining camps where work and pay were inconsistent. Women often had to take in boarders, cook and clean for other families and barter to keep things going. In Kevin Anderson's article "Sedor Fedukovich: A New American in Fayette County," he writes:

> *While grandpa was away working in the mines, Grandma kept the garden, hoeing the corn and potatoes and pulling weeds....Grandma was an exceptional baker, and the miners where grandpa worked soon knew it. She routinely baked rolls and biscuits for him to take to the mines to be sold. For many years she used an old wood or coal burning stove for*

her cooking. In addition to her baked goods, she sold eggs and frying-size rabbits for extra income.

When the Great Depression began in 1929, West Virginia had already experienced almost ten years of economic crisis. The rapid increase in industry in West Virginia led to a need for infrastructure and public services. West Virginia issued bonds for roads, schools and new construction, but the people in the state, many already living hand to mouth, were outraged at government spending and put a stop to it. The lack of infrastructure was a main factor in not being able to bring in other industries even as the coal industry declined due to overdevelopment and mechanization.

For generations in West Virginia, free-range grazing was a way for indigenous farmers to raise livestock without growing or buying feed. The hogs they rounded up and slaughtered in the fall gave them a meaningful product not only to consume in the home but also to use to barter and trade in an area where money was scarce. The extractive industries took a heavy toll on the "commons" concept that encouraged free-range grazing. Mining and timbering polluted water, clear-cut forests and forced farmers to fence their livestock on their property. Making matters worse was the loss of the main source of mast for free-range hogs when the blight wiped out the American chestnut. The situation worsened when a devastating drought in 1929 affected both livestock and crop cultivation. Farmers were broke and could not borrow money to buy equipment, seeds or fertilizers and spray. In Janet Greene's article "Women's Work in the Southern West Virginia Coal Camps," she writes:

> *In times when families moved frequently or during strikes, maintaining a garden and preserving the produce was impossible. During the Depression of the 1930s these clandestine gardens became more important for residents of the coal camps, especially for black and foreign-born families, who owned no "home place" or small farm in the mountains to return to when the mines were not working. These gardens were especially important to black families because more than 90 percent of the black mining population of the southern West Virginia coalfields lived in company housing.*

Men took whatever jobs they could find, often under dangerous conditions, like building Union Carbide's Hawk's Nest Tunnel. The tunnel was filled with silicosis, and between 800 and 1,500 men died from acute silicosis. It remains one of the worst American industrial accidents to date.

Dwight Harshbarger's book *Witness at Hawks Nest* describes the living conditions of the camps:

> *Men slept in segregated shanties. The workers were not allowed to cook due to fire hazards. Mess hall with segregated tables where they ate bean soup, cheese sandwiches and sweet tea. Local diners popped up to service the workers and they served blue plate specials: beef patties, roast beef with gravy, mashed potatoes, green beans with bacon, biscuits, chocolate cake and mile high pie.*

When reflecting on the hard times of the Depression in an interview in *Goldenseal* magazine, Francis Upton Custer remarked:

> *Farmers had a hard time due to high taxes. Grain and livestock feed were expensive compared to what they made at market when they sold their products. Below average rainfall did not help crops. I think the main foods eaten by most people were dried beans, potatoes and bread. We raised large gardens and canned surplus vegetables. We also canned fruit. My father butchered hogs in the fall....I remember menus printed by the government that allowed 20 cents a day per person. This is about what I spent.*

The Works Progress Administration (WPA) was a New Deal program created by the Franklin D. Roosevelt administration to employ millions of otherwise unemployed workers on public work projects of all types, including building much of the infrastructure still in use at Coopers Rock State Park and around the state. Able-bodied men like Lowell Brookover of Harrison County joined the WPA program not only for employment but also to gain skills.

First Lady Eleanor Roosevelt visited the Scotts Run area and was so horrified at the conditions she saw that she created a homestead community named Arthurdale that relocated 165 (mainly native white West Virginians) to Preston County. They were given homes with a few acres to garden and plant fruit trees. Each family also had a root cellar. Two other homestead communities, Tygart Valley and Eleanor, were also developed by the first lady. Although not considered a great success, they did give many families a chance at a new life.

Walking to town for relief during the Depression. *Library of Congress.*

The immigrants brought in to work low-paying, hard jobs in the mines arrived with different languages, cultural beliefs and customs that many locals considered strange or intimidating. These differences also held immigrants back from economic opportunities. In an attempt to remedy these conditions, Americanization programs were launched by both local and national relief agencies, including the Red Cross, the American Friends Service Committee and Presbyterian and Methodist home missions. These programs included sewing, cooking, food preservation and gardening classes; charm school; and Bible school, and they also supplied healthcare and food assistance. In general, however, the immigrants themselves had a strong desire to assimilate and take advantage of what America had to offer, and they and their descendants prospered and contributed mightily to the nation. Even as they assimilated, the immigrants still impacted West Virginia foodways by varying degrees. For instance, Luis Arego wrote in *Goldenseal* magazine that among the immigrants from the Asturian region of Spain who often found work in zinc mining, "where Asturian immigrants were in the majority, [there were] places where for many years people could speak the

101

Asturian language, ate fabada (mixture of beans and rice with chicken), played the bagpipe, and danced the traditional Xiringüelu for fun."

Polish immigrants brought with them the pierogi, a boiled dumpling, which in time became a popular mainstream dish, as did cabbage rolls, which were a Hungarian specialty. Jewish immigrants arriving in coal camps often struggled to obtain kosher foods but persevered in their efforts to remain observant.

As the dominant ethnic group of immigrants, the Italians likewise dominated the shift in West Virginia's foodways. As the group was overwhelmingly composed of people from the southern provinces of Italy, their dishes reflect the simplicity of authentic Italian cooking, which relies on quality ingredients. The traditional spaghetti, linguine or fettucine served up at dinner was often handmade using a *chitarra* (a wooden device with wire strings like a guitar through which pasta dough could be pushed and cut into long ribbons that would then be hung up and dried around the house). Ravioli, stuffed with cheese and perhaps veal, would also be handmade and were often served at Easter. The traditional red sauce was usually somewhat *arrabbiata* (spicy, with a little heat) and not so sweet as one might encounter in a modern chain restaurant. Experts can argue where and when the pizza was born, but regardless it became very popular around the state. Pizzas were often rectangular in shape and could fit in shirt boxes as opposed to the popular image of the round pizza. Italian meats and cheeses leapt from the immigrants' tables to the mainstream, no doubt enticing new consumers when they were prominently displayed in the windows of the many Italian groceries that populated mining communities around the state. Red wine was always on the table and usually made at home.

World War II started on September 1, 1939, and lasted until September 2, 1945. The war ended the Great Depression and had a profound effect on the lives of Americans and West Virginians. Many women went to work during the war, changing the dynamic of the family as well as what they ate. The consumption of convenience food increased during this period, as did ethnic cuisine. In the wake of World War II, West Virginia evolved much like the rest of America. Women had found jobs in the factories, and many were not inclined to return to the status quo. Advances in transportation and mass communications did much to connect West Virginia to the outside world. Good-paying job opportunities in factories in states like Ohio and Michigan led to yet another exodus of residents but at the same time created a path between the states that would affect all of their cultures.

Advances in food storage, appliances and food itself affected the state just as they did the rest of the country. The pace of life was picking up, and the old, slow ways of gathering and preparing food were often rejected in favor of the quick, the easy and the economical. West Virginians were not immune to the siren songs of Madison Avenue, which was incessantly pitching freeze-dried this and prepackaged that on television, radio and in print. West Virginia kids wanted to drink Tang because the astronauts did, and when the microwave oven appeared, it swiftly made its way into West Virginia households.

The era of the chain restaurant took hold after the war. People—in particular travelers—were eager to trade unique, homegrown eating establishments for the comfort of sameness and at least the illusion of better prices. Some of the chains thrived and survived—McDonald's, Burger King, KFC and Pizza Hut—while others ultimately disappeared. The Shoney's restaurant chain was founded in West Virginia by Alex Schoenbaum in 1947. Today, there are more than two hundred locations in sixteen states.

Even into the 1970s, much of West Virginia had what were known as blue laws, which, among other things, often forbade businesses to be open on Sundays. But as the laws were repealed and new interstate highways were completed, the opportunity to offer services seven days a week was too enticing to pass up. As for the towns the highways bypassed, they often shrank, losing restaurants that couldn't compete with shiny new chains dominating the exits. There was a token "back-to-the-land" movement in the '70s, but it seemed to flicker and die under the tidal wave of disco and the rise of Wall Street.

By the late twentieth century, West Virginia was home to the ubiquitous chain restaurants and shops that dominate the rest of the American landscape. Gas stations ceased to focus on fuel and abandoned service as they mutated into combination convenience store/fast-food joints. Convenience and conformity replaced home-cooked and unique. Industrial-scale agricultural operations displaced the family farm.

In spite of all this massive change to the state and its people, there was something happening to counter the race to the generic. West Virginia's foods and cultures were about to stage a comeback.

❖ ❖ ❖

Pepperoni Rolls

1 package active dry yeast
¼ cup warm water
1 cup milk, scalded
1 teaspoon salt
¼ cup sugar
¼ cup shortening
3½ cups flour, sifted
1 egg
1 large stick of pepperoni roll cut into smaller sticks

Soften yeast in warm water. In a pan, scald the milk and add salt, sugar and shortening. When that cools off, add half the flour and mix in yeast and egg. Gradually add remaining flour and form a soft dough. Place in a greased bowl. Let dough rise, work down and rise again. Pinch off small amount and roll out. Fold over pepperoni piece and press the edges closed. Place on pan pressed side down. Cover and let rise. Bake at 400 degrees for 15 to 20 minutes. Butter the tops while still hot.

❈ ❈ ❈

Pepperoni Rolls

1 pack Rhodes Frozen Dough, dinner roll size
1 stick pepperoni

Let pack of dough defrost in the refrigerator overnight. If the pepperoni has a thick paper cover, peel it off. Cut into chunks, then grind up in the food processor in a few small batches. Roll out dough, place a spoonful of pepperoni in the middle, fold over and press edges together. Place on greased baking sheet and let rise for about an hour. Bake at 400 degrees for 15 to 20 minutes and butter fresh from the oven.

❈ ❈ ❈

Fairmont-Style Hot Dog Sauce

From Bob Heffner's Pepperoni Roll homepage.

1 C. finely chopped onion
5 pounds ground beef
¼ pound ground pork
1 T. black pepper
1 T. salt
3 T. chili powder
4 T. crushed red chili pepper (medium hot)
1 32 oz. can tomato sauce
1 14 or 15 oz. bottle ketchup
1 small can tomato paste
1 T. olive oil
¼ t. cumin
1 dash Tabasco sauce

In a large pot, sauté the onion in the olive oil until tender but not browned. Crumble the raw hamburger and ground pork and add to the pot. Cover with water and cook for 1 hour, uncovered, adding more water if necessary. Add the remaining ingredients and cook, covered, over low heat, just simmering, for two more hours.

If you wish a thinner sauce, add more water halfway through the final two hours. For thick sauce, cook down, uncovered for a while longer.

This recipe makes quite a lot of hot dog sauce, so we freeze it in small lots and then microwave to thaw. This is not called Chili around here; it's Hot Dog Sauce and this style of sauce, or some variation of it is found in all of the dog stands in this town and in most of North Central West Virginia.

❖ ❖ ❖

Coleslaw

1 head cabbage, finely shredded
1 medium onion, shredded
1 cup sugar
1 cup vinegar
½ cup vegetable salad oil
¼ cup water
1 teaspoon mustard from a jar
¼ cup salad dressing
1 cup vinegar
1 teaspoon celery seed
1 ½ teaspoons salt

Shred one head of cabbage and the onion. Place in a bowl and add 1 cup of sugar. In a pan, combine other ingredients and bring to a boil for 3 minutes. Pour over cabbage mixture and refrigerate.

❖ ❖ ❖

Calamari in Spicy Tomato Sauce (for Feast of the Seven Fishes)

⅓ cup olive oil
3 carrots, minced
1 stalk celery, minced
1 onion, minced
3 cloves garlic, minced
3 anchovy fillets, rinsed and minced
¼ cup white wine or stock
3 large cans crushed tomatoes
Salt and pepper to taste
Hot pepper flakes
1–2 pounds calamari, cleaned and cut up
Fresh parsley
Fresh basil

Heat oil at low/medium in pot. Add minced carrots, celery and onion and sauté until tender. Add the garlic last and cook until soft. Do not let it burn. Add the anchovies and cook until they dissolve. Add the wine and let the alcohol cook off. Add the crushed tomatoes. Then add salt and pepper and hot pepper flakes; this is a "feel" thing. Don't go crazy at first—after the sauce has cooked, you can always add more to taste. Add the calamari to the sauce and simmer for at least 2 hours. Stir occasionally to make sure it doesn't burn. Chop up the fresh herbs and add at the end of cooking. Toss over cooked pasta.

Chapter 6
THE FUTURE OF
WEST VIRGINIA FOOD

In spite of its legendary lack of accessibility, West Virginia has nonetheless found itself repeatedly at or near the epicenter of American history from colonial times through the Revolution, from pioneer days and the Civil War through the Industrial Revolution, the melting pot of immigration and the rise and fall of the Rust Belt. And as we have seen, the state's foodways were shaped by and responded to all of those pivotal events. And now, in the early twenty-first century, those foodways are enjoying a renaissance and impacting the state in ways that are as important as before, if not more so.

Of course, West Virginia now offers more choice to diners. Even small towns in the interior can boast of Chinese restaurants. Sushi bars may be found in larger cities, along with other exotic offerings from cultures around the world. And West Virginia is not exempt from the rise of the chain restaurant. In fact, the state is even home to two: Tudor's Biscuit World and Geno's Pizza & Spaghetti. But what's really exciting in the state is a little more homegrown.

For all its uniqueness of landscape and culture, West Virginia nonetheless has much in common with other states and is not immune to national or regional trends. As most, if not all, American states found their farming population reduced, family farms disappearing and large agribusiness interests taking their place, so did these things occur in West Virginia. But in the last few decades, there has been a revival of interest in food—where it comes from, how it's grown, how it's prepared. Part of this interest derives from a desire to eat healthier, part of it may be in response to concern about corporate control of food and part of it may just be a heartfelt desire to enjoy great culinary experiences—or perhaps a combination of all three. The phrase "farm-to-table" may have become somewhat overused in the recent past, but it is in fact a concise way of describing the desire to eat food that is grown locally, safely, as organically as possible and with elements of heirloom varieties of plants as well as meat and dairy products and also foraged foods. West Virginia has a long history as a tourist destination, and now, in addition to our natural beauty, historical sites, cultural arts and outdoor adventure activities, our foods and foodways are being sought out by culinary adventurers from within and out of the state's borders.

Let's start by looking at what's happening with farming in the Mountain State. Beginning in the late 1990s, there began to be a noticeable surge in cities and towns hosting local farmers' markets. The response by the public was instantaneous, and enthusiasm grew. Eventually, cities like Charleston and Morgantown developed dedicated spaces for the markets. A summer Saturday morning will find the large outdoor covered space crowded with throngs of shoppers who can pick up not only locally grown produce but also eggs; honey; fresh-baked bread; free-range beef, lamb, chicken and pork; and seasonal offerings like ramps or maple syrup.

In Charleston, the Capital Market was developed from an old train station, and the result is nothing short of spectacular, combining daily offerings of produce by regional farmers outside with a variety of stands offering prepared foods and other items on the inside. Huntington is home to the Wild Ramp, "a year-round, non-profit farmers market…with a mission to grow and support a vibrant economy and community for local food, food products and artisan goods." According to the West Virginia Farmers Market Association, there were only 34 West Virginia farmers' markets in 2005. That number has jumped to 120. From Point Marketplace in Parkersburg to the historic Centre Market in Wheeling (operating since the early 1850s) to Lewisburg to Charles Town to the Almost Heaven Farmer's Market in Bluefield and many, many points in between, farmers' markets have exploded, proving there was a market for quality foods and for the fellowship and entertainment such gatherings can generate.

The rise of farmers' markets in turn sent a message to the state's farmers and folks who thought they might like to give farming a try. This is where the story gets interesting and a little tougher to consolidate, as there are so many examples of what the farm-to-table movement has unleashed.

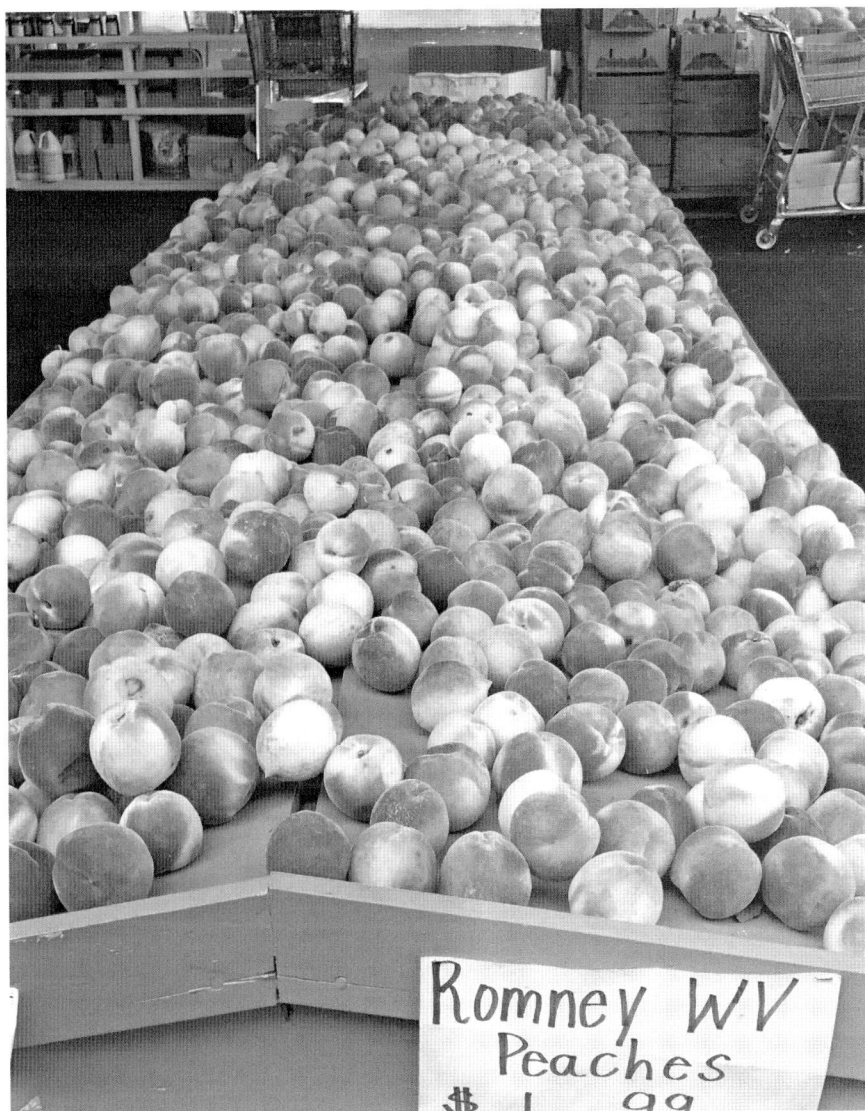

West Virginia is home to many farms and orchards. Peaches are a favorite, especially the famous Greenbrier peaches. *West Virginia Farmers Market Association.*

Existing farm operations, like Gritt's Farm in Buffalo and Orr's Farm Market near Martinsburg, saw the rise in interest in local food and farming and responded. For both operations, that meant acknowledging the interactive experience folks were craving; pick-your-own berry and fruit opportunities were developed and promoted. Schoolchildren in particular have been the beneficiaries of the pick-your-own experience. But the expansion of farm operations went beyond pick-your-own and included on-site farm markets and, in the case of Gritt's, CSAs (community-supported agriculture), which customers can "subscribe" to and pick up seasonal produce weekly. The larger, existing farms were not the only ones to recognize the opportunities renewed interest in food and farming represented.

Around the state, in numbers too large to be accounted for here, farming operations sprouted up, often reflecting specialization in crops. For example, Evans Knob Farm, in northeastern Preston County, has operated consistently since 2003 utilizing organic practices and has even gone beyond the basics of organic certification. In addition to CSA memberships and farmers' market participation, it offers customers pastured poultry and grass-fed lamb.

Far to the south, in Greenbrier County, Mountain Top Farm began as a pick-your-own berry operation but has evolved to offer a more complete line of produce, including pumpkins. You may recall a quote earlier in the book about corn crops being greatly damaged by cold and wet and striking fear into the hearts of farmers. In an effort to combat that uncertainty, like many operations, large and small, throughout the state, Mountain Top has developed high and low tunnels to extend the growing season, thereby combating the erratic nature of weather.

In Upshur County, Fish Hawk Acres has emerged as a truly branded farming/food operation whose website boasts of "a farm, a Market a unique Cafe and a wildly popular custom catering service....Fish Hawk Acres provides fresh food sourced locally and regionally." Additionally, co-owner and chef Dale Hawkins has emerged as a leading figure in West Virginia's culinary scene and, among other accomplishments, hosted the *Appalachian Food Evangelist* television cooking show, which reflected his passionate interest in foods and foodways of the region, as well as healthy farming practices.

The West Virginia Department of Agriculture also developed a West Virginia Farm to School program that works to increase the amount of locally grown food served in school lunch programs. It also works on developing and educating the next generation of West Virginia farmers. The West Virginia Department of Education's Farm to School program has similar missions.

Of course, not every farm is large and profitable. In fact, according to the West Virginia Department of Agriculture, "West Virginia's agriculture community is made up primarily of small family owned and operated farms. Approximately 80 percent of the Mountain State's 20,600 farms have income of less than $10,000."

The opportunities brought about by America's renewed interest in food and foodways did not only spark innovation and expansion in for-profit farming. Around the state, nonprofit cooperatives and community efforts came to life in support of public health and the potential for increased employment.

For example, in South Charleston, a community garden has been established at the historic but now closed Rock Lake pool site. Once the largest pool of its kind in the United States, the site is now owned by Rock Lake Presbyterian Church, which donated space for the community garden to Manna Meals, a nonprofit soup kitchen and pantry whose volunteers plant, water and harvest produce from the garden. In 2015, Manna Meals served over 150,000 meals to those in need. The organization has also started a children's program that educates kids on how to grow food and where food comes from.

The Wayne County Farmers Cooperative exists to create agricultural jobs in an area of high unemployment. Education is a cornerstone of the coop, as they teach participants beekeeping, mushroom cultivation, maple syrup production and how to grow produce. They also are converting available unused land to agricultural use, and that includes building high and low tunnels that are unheated, plastic covered structures used to grow and protect plants and extend growing seasons.

Grow Ohio Valley, in the Wheeling area, is a particularly inspiring group that has identified a number of goals and initiatives, including the development of vacant lots into community gardens; working with school cafeterias to promote serving vegetables from schoolyard gardens and local farms; and widespread access to low-cost, healthy vegetables, even in low-income neighborhoods.

The West Virginia State Department of Agriculture has not stood idly by while the farm-to-table movement evolved in the state. In fact, the department has for years, and under different administrations, worked hard to assist and develop farming opportunities in the Mountain State, particularly in service to the need to diversify an economy that has for over a century been focused on extractive industries like mining. One area the department identified as having great potential for success involved the state's veterans. West Virginia has historically contributed a percentage of enlistees in the armed forces higher than the national average. And with the recent conflicts in the Middle East, there were many veterans returning home and searching for opportunities. With that in mind, the department launched the Veterans and Warriors to Agriculture Program. This multifaceted initiative not only

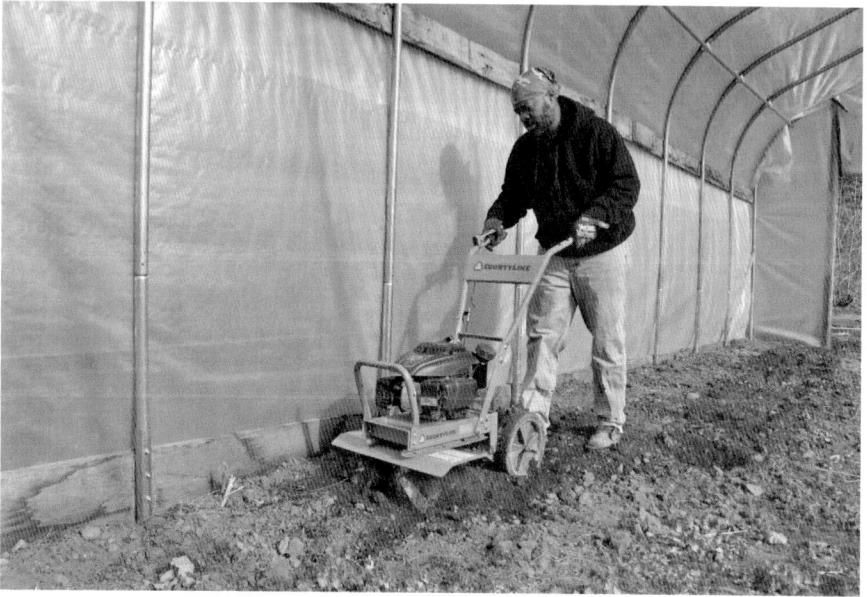

The West Virginia Veterans Program in McDowell County grows a variety of produce and educates local youths about agriculture. *West Virginia Department of Agriculture.*

assists veterans who either farm or are interested in farming with education, research and product and brand development and promotion but also seeks to creative therapeutic benefits through agricultural activities.

Among the vets who have participated and found success within the program is Calvin Riggleman. After his service in Iraq in 2003 and 2005, Riggleman returned home to farm in Pleasant Dale. He has developed a great number of products under the Bigg Riggs brand that qualify for the Homegrown by Heroes label (a designation of the Farmer-Veteran Coalition) and has great success at Washington, D.C.–area farmers' markets, which are a reasonable drive from West Virginia's eastern panhandle. In a reflection of the need to be diversified in order to survive and prosper in the modern agricultural world, he has developed several aspects of his operation, including CSAs, a canning and labeling operation open to other farmers and value-added products like Bigg Riggs Awesome Sauce—which really is awesome.

Another area of agriculture the West Virginia Department of Agriculture has identified and worked to support is specialty crops. Through a series of grants, the department supports state farmers who are working to develop crops that fall outside what might be termed "commodity crops" (examples would be corn, soybeans and sorghum). Specialty crops can include fruits, vegetables, tree nuts, maple syrup, nursery crops and even Christmas trees.

Glancing quickly over the list, maple syrup may come as a surprise, as it is so identifiable with New England. But West Virginia has more tappable maple trees than Vermont, which is the leading maple syrup producer in the United States. Since early settlers came into the area and learned to tap the maple trees from the Indians, maple syrup has been a staple in West Virginia. The art of making maple syrup remained the same, and that old-time tradition was practiced in West Virginia. Maple syrup is made from tapping several varieties of maples but primarily the sugar maple. The trees are usually tapped on a warm day after a freezing spell. As the season progresses, the sap becomes darker in color and stronger in flavor. Maple syrup comes from the boiled-down sap of the sugar maple tree. Each year in early spring, maple producers, also called "sugar makers," head to their woods for the start of maple syrup season, which generally lasts from mid-February to early April. Maple producers "tap," or drill, a small hole into the trunk of a tree and then insert a spout or spile to catch the sap that begins to collect in the hole. Traditionally, the spout was connected to a bucket to collect the dripping sap. Once the sap starts collecting in the bucket, it needs to be processed right away.

Sugar makers use evaporators to make maple syrup. An evaporator consists of two or more large specially designed pans that are filled with sap. These pans sit over a fire of burning wood or some other fuel, which heats the sap and causes it to boil. As it boils, some of the water in the sap turns to steam, which rises out of the sugarhouse. The sap becomes thicker and sweeter. The sugar maker has to watch the boiling sap very carefully because it could easily burn in the evaporator. As the sap thickens, it gets hotter. The sugar maker knows the maple syrup is ready when its temperature reaches seven degrees Fahrenheit above the boiling point of water. This process requires a lot of time and energy because it takes between forty to fifty gallons of sap to make just one gallon of pure maple syrup. Once the maple syrup is thick enough, it is filtered to take out "sugar sand," which accumulates as sap boils. Sugar sand is just minerals and nutrients that concentrate as the excess water is boiled away. If it is not filtered out, the maple syrup will appear cloudy.

One of the emerging successful maple tapping operations, Heasley Homestead Maple, near Bruceton Mills, is a great place to visit in-season. The owners tap around seven hundred trees and employ a reverse-osmosis method that allows the syrup to be processed more efficiently, even prior to evaporation. Their syrup is tasty and healthy; as noted on their website, maple is a healthy alternative to artificial sweeteners. It contains numerous antioxidants and supplies important vitamins and minerals, including zinc, manganese, potassium and calcium.

The many efforts the West Virginia Department of Agriculture and like-minded organizations and institutions like the West Virginia Farm Bureau, the WVU Extension Service and the NRCS/USDA perform on behalf of West Virginia's farmers and consumers are too detailed to explore within the confines of this book, but there is one further area that deserves deeper examination: agritourism and tourism that is at least partially driven by culinary appreciation.

Tourism in general has been one of the state's economic strengths dating back to the colonial era and the development of the "baths" in the eastern panhandle. From the soaring, rugged beauty of Seneca Rocks to the engineering marvel that is the New River Gorge Bridge to the fascinating Ohio River Island Wildlife Refuge, from Civil War historical sites in Harpers Ferry to the scuba diving destination offered up by Summersville Lake, and hundreds of points in between, West Virginia is blessed with natural, historical and cultural attractions. Kayakers, mountain bikers, rock climbers, fishermen, hunters, bird watchers and white-water rafters are among the many outdoor enthusiasts drawn to the state. Whatever their reasons for coming initially, these folks all have something in common: they must eat. Combine that basic need with the farm-to-table phenomenon and you come away with opportunity.

At the most basic level, pick-your-own operations, farm tours and onsite farm markets, along with community farmers' markets, are the bedrock of agritourism. But there are larger examples in play. A prime example would be the Heritage Farm Museum and Village near Huntington. Its official description bears repeating here: "The Heritage Farm Museum and Village has won many awards over the years, most notably recognized as a National Geographic Traveler Prime Destination, Daughters of the American Revolution Medal for Historic Preservation, and selected as the site for two History Channel features, 'America's Greatest Feud' Hatfield McCoy Documentary and 'American Pickers.'"

Today, the farm's collection includes more than twenty-five thousand square feet of Appalachian artifacts in seven museums dedicated to Progress, Industry, Transportation, Children's Activity, Bowe's Doll and Carriage, Country Store and Heritage Museum. Recently named West

West Virginia has always had a strong agricultural background; 95 percent of farms in West Virginia are family owned—the highest percentage in the United States. *Mike Forte.*

Virginia's first Smithsonian Affiliate Institution, the property is also home to more than thirty structures, including two reception halls for up to three hundred people; five log cabin inns; a Barn Retreat Center that sleeps forty people, wired with today's technology; and overnight train-caboose accommodations.

Artisans and reenactors bring Appalachian history to life during special Way Back Weekends on Saturdays in May through December, when thousands of people from around the world learn from the past, appreciate today and dream for the future. With over five hundred acres, five miles of hiking trails, artisan workshops and new attractions on the horizon, Heritage Farm Museum and Village is proudly positioned to serve Appalachia for many years to come.

Fairs and festivals also represent significant attractors of tourists interested in West Virginia foods and foodways, and that includes native foods that are the result of foraging as opposed to cultivation. Of course, there are the large state and county fairs, but it is in the smaller events that the pursuit of authenticity and local foods can perhaps best be realized. West Virginia's longest-running heritage celebration, Mountain State Art and Craft Fair in Ripley, has a rich tradition of celebrating and preserving the diverse cultures that populate Appalachia through arts, crafts and food. Nicholas County has a potato festival, Preston County celebrates buckwheat and the Mountain State Apple Festival calls Martinsburg home. Richwood's Feast of the Ramson celebrates the ramp (as do myriad local "ramp dinners" across the state) and Spencer in Roane County has the Black Walnut Festival, and who can forget Pocahontas County's WV RoadKill Cookoff and Autumn Harvest Festival. There are festivals dedicated to strawberries, blackberries, chocolate, wine, chestnuts, honey, craft brews and more. There are also festivals centered on ethnic foods. Clarksburg's Italian Heritage Festival draws tens of thousands of attendees every year as it celebrates the contributions of Italian immigrants to the region's prosperity, culture and cuisine. In neighboring Fairmont, every December, the Feast of the Seven Fishes Festival brings thousands downtown in a celebration aimed at preserving the traditional Christmas Eve seafood meal, complete with a cooking school. Clarksburg is also home to the West Virginia Black Heritage Festival, while the African American Cultural Heritage Festival is celebrated in Jefferson County. Both festivals strive to preserve and promote African American culture. In Helvetia, the tiny community's Swiss roots are celebrated with Fasnacht. For over eighty years in Wheeling, the Mahrajan, a Lebanese festival, has been inviting visitors from all cultures to sample tabbouleh, pita bread, hummus, stuffed grape leaves, baked kibbeh and other authentic dishes.

As we have seen since the earliest days of settlement, the processing of things like corn into "value-added" products diversified and augmented farmers' livelihood. Now, as then, the opportunity of creating "hard spirits" from locally grown foods has grown to be a thriving niche in the West Virginia culinary scene. It all started with the relaxing of laws governing home brewing and distilling practices, which was in turn a reaction to the exploding national interest in craft beers, wine and spirits.

Discerning tourists (and locals for that matter) are often passionate about their beverage of choice, and West Virginia purveyors of craft spirits have responded. Let's start with beer. It seems logical to expect some presence of craft brewing in areas that attract outdoor sports enthusiasts, and that logic is borne out in places like Tucker County and Fayetteville. In the former, visitors to Canaan and Timberline ski areas; to the towns of Davis and Thomas and their charming arts and cultural scenes; and to the natural beauty of Blackwater Falls and Canaan Valley and the hiking, biking, kayaking, fishing and other sports on hand are fortunate to have

Mountain State Brewing, Blackwater Brewing and Stumptown Ales close at hand to deliver an assortment of craft beers (not to mention great coffee; Thomas's Tip Top has been cited by the *Washington Post* for its great coffee selection). Fayetteville draws an enormous number of white-water rafters, rock climbers and others, many of whom seek out Bridge Brew Works. The craft brew scene is not limited to resort/adventure areas, however, and establishments can be found around the state—from Short Story Brewing in Rivesville to Big Timber in Elkins. Wheeling, Charleston, Beckley, Parkersburg, Morgantown, Huntington, Lewisburg, Summersville, Charles Town, Berkeley Springs and even tiny Cuzzart can boast of breweries—and more are popping up all the time. Festival activities are also growing around the craft beer scene, including the West Virginia Craft Brew Fest in Greenbrier County. A random sampling of the beers on tap around the Mountain State reveals an eclectic and rewarding list to choose from. Dolly Suds Cranberry Wheat (Mountain State), Hellbender Black IPA (Bridge Brew Works), Mothman Black IPA (Greenbrier Valley Brewing), Wildflower Honey Wit (the Peddler, Huntington), Roedy's Red (North End, Parkersburg), Eireann Dearg Irish Red (Wheeling's Brew Keepers) and the Sour Kid (Weathered Ground, Beckley) are just a handful of the dozens of craft beers offered up across the state.

While beer may dominate the modern drinking scene, there was a time in West Virginia when it was not so. In fact, hard apple cider was often the drink of choice. Josh Bennett, owner of Hawk Knob Cidery and Meadery in Greenbrier County, is dedicated to creating heritage barrel-aged ciders, using locally sourced apples as much as possible. Visitors to the Hawk Knob tasting room are often surprised at the complexity of the ciders and the realization that they represent a viable alternative to wine, not only in taste but in the fact that West Virginia is very conducive to apple cultivation. Over in Pendleton County, another cider company, Swilled Dog, has emerged and is gaining popularity throughout the state.

Wineries are tailor-made for agritourism and are one of the most visible manifestations of the farm-to-table movement. What was once the provenance of France and California's Napa Valley has spread throughout the United States. In addition to the wine itself, the vineyards attached to a winery lend a picturesque quality that smart vintners capitalize on to attract customers who are looking for something more than just tasting and purchasing. West Virginia has several wineries that have recognized this and put those practices to good use. The vineyard at Forks of Cheat Winery in Monongalia County spills over a hillside near

Cheat Lake and is a frequent site for weddings, as is Heston's Winery in neighboring Marion County. From its beginnings in 1992, Lambert's Winery in Lewis County has developed a gorgeous setting with cellars constructed of enormous cut stones, beautiful grounds and a catering service. West-Whitehill Winery in Moorefield makes a compelling case for its wines: "From French-American hybrid varietals selected to withstand the colder climate of the eastern Alleghanies. Located in Hardy County in the eastern panhandle, the South Branch Valley lies in a unique 'rain shadow,' which receives less rain than anywhere else in the state, making it more ideal for growing grapes than surrounding areas." Daniel Vineyards (Crab Orchard) is another sought-after event site, as is Chestnut Ridge Winery in Roane County (which even offers its own blend of tea). While Stone Road Vineyards (Wirt County), Potomac Highlands Winery (Mineral County) and DeFeo Family Vineyard and Winery (Ripley) are all dedicated to perfecting their unique vintages, Kirkwood Winery in Nicholas County has expanded beyond wine in a move toward the earliest days of West Virginia's settlement. It opened a distillery.

The late Rodney Facemire, along with his partner, Shirley Morris, labored and lobbied hard to make the distillery a reality. And even after receiving a license to operate what is quite possibly the smallest licensed distillery in America, they still faced an uphill battle in that they could sell licensed spirits through retailers but the Isaiah Morgan products (according to their website) "couldn't be sold at the site of their creation, disappointing many tourists. Rodney conceived the vision of mini-distilleries, formed a team of government and business leaders and created what can become a new industry for the state." Facemire was right to recognize the tourism component's value to small hard-spirit operations, and his vision has been proven right. Visitors to Isaiah Morgan can purchase small-batch corn liquor and rye whiskeys, as well as grappa.

The Hatfield and McCoy saga is perhaps West Virginia's most-recognized contribution to the American story. These days, off-road enthusiasts flock to the Hatfield-McCoy Trails, one of the largest off-highway vehicle trail systems in the world, with over six hundred miles of maintained trails that course through Logan, Kanawha, Wyoming, McDowell, Mercer, Wayne, Lincoln, Mingo and Boone Counties—the same rugged country that was the site of the epic family feud. It seems only right that the region should be home to distilleries—and in fact it is. Hatfield and McCoy Moonshine is crafted in small batches at the distillery site in Gilbert from a recipe handed down from "Devil Anse" Hatfield himself. Mountain Mama Moonshine offers up an inviting tasting room in the town of Man, not far from the trail. Head east to Greenbrier County, and you'll find Smooth Ambler Distillery, whose motto is "Patiently Made Appalachian Whiskey." What you'll also find is a commitment to sourcing ingredients locally. When you sip the rye whiskey, chances are good the rye was grown there in the Greenbrier Valley.

The growing passion for authentic, healthy foods and foodways is nowhere more evident than in the growing number of restaurants around the state that offer up genuine alternatives to generic chain restaurant fare. Sourcing locally, adjusting the menu seasonally and creating unique, inviting atmospheres is a bedrock commonality of these purveyors of "Appalachian cuisine," and their numbers are growing. A quick survey of some of the menu items offered at a variety of restaurants around the state offers up a snapshot of the creativity and ethos at work.

Charleston's Bluegrass Kitchen's menu features a diverse offering of farm-to-table foods with a modern twist. How about starting with smoked poblano stuffed with West Virginia's Spring Gap Creamery cheddar and cream cheese, topped with green tomato chow-chow, crème fraiche and served with corn chips, and then following up with trout with grits? This might be a good time to mention that the salt on the table comes from the nearby J.Q. Dickinson's revived saltworks—another great culinary tourism destination.

Not far from the Bluegrass is Sumthin' Good Soul Food, which reflects owner Denise Jones's passion for recipes handed down from her ancestors and named for them. So don't be surprised to find Grandma Shirley's Cabbage and Momma Fran's Candied Yams on the menu.

The Stardust Café, in Lewisburg, strives to provide foods that are not only sourced locally but also reflect the values of sustainability and the free trade movement. And it has an arugula and chevre burger featuring local beef, which isn't hard to come by when you have acclaimed growers of grass-fed beef nearby at places like Swift Level Farm.

Just about dead center in the state, in the town of Sutton, Chef Tim Urbanic and his family and staff run the acclaimed Café Cimino. The location might be small-town and rural, but the menu is anything but. For two decades, Urbanic has worked to fuse his Italian heritage and culinary influences with locally sourced ingredients—many of which he grows on his farm. And when ramps are in season, ramps are on the table.

If you find yourself in Morgantown, delightful establishments like Tin 202 and Table 9 are devoted to a like-minded approach to cuisine, as is Hill and Hollow. Chef M.K. Ohlinger's innovative Appalachian cuisine has resulted in a menu that features a dizzying array of imaginative dishes such as pork cracklins with a roasted scallions citrus dip, cornmeal-encrusted walleye pike with ramp remoulade and pan-fried veal sweetbreads with pistachio pesto pasta. That menu also lists dozens of area farms, bakeries, craft breweries and other businesses that enable the restaurant to source as local, fresh and authentic to the region as possible.

You can start with garlic truffle fries at the Vagabond Kitchen in Wheeling, while in Shepherdstown, at Domestic, you can enjoy blackened catfish with cheddar grits. Or sample desserts at the Station in Fayetteville, including vanilla bean panna cotta and peanut butter pie. And if you are "taking the waters" at the historic baths in Berkeley Springs, consider the panko-crusted cauliflower-zucchini "linguine" with roasted tomato coulis and fresh mozzarella at Lot 12 Public House.

As important and exciting as the farm-to-table movement is, it is by no means the only culinary draw West Virginia has to offer. Of course, for locals there are always landmarks that have been enjoyed by families for generations, each with its own history and stories to tell. Just ask the locals. Chances are good that in New Martinsville, they'll recommend Quinet's. Jim's Restaurant (Huntington), King Tut's Drive-In (Beckley), Biggie's (Grafton), Boyd's Steakhouse (Martinsburg) and Austin's Ice Cream (Ceredo) are icons of their communities.

A great example is Cool Springs, near Rowlesburg in Preston County. Prior to the coming of the interstates, Route 50 was the way to travel from West Virginia to Washington, D.C., as well as points west. Cool Springs, like myriad other such businesses, developed to offer auto travelers and tourists fuel, food, groceries, a gift shop and grounds that invite visitors to picnic, explore old train and farm equipment, watch farm animals mill around and browse bins of apples and other produce for sale. Inside, the legendary footlong hot dogs still tempt diners. Even as other such businesses along Route 50 have disappeared, Cool Springs still draws a steady stream of visitors and is one of West Virginia's hidden gems.

Hillbilly Hotdogs, which made an appearance on Food Network's *Diners, Drive-Ins and Dives*, in Lesage is not as old as Cool Springs, but it sure feels like a classic tourist stop of bygone days. Motorcycle enthusiasts are among the many customers you'll find crowding the parking lot in search of an unbelievable variety of hot dogs. Then again, tiny Yann's Hot Dogs up in Fairmont may not sport a gift shop, or even regular business hours these days, but the delightfully spicy meat sauce has a huge and devoted following.

North-central West Virginia, as we know, is home to a large Italian American immigrant population and several long-established restaurants with passionate fan bases. Minard's, Oliverio's, Muriale's, Julio's, the Wonder Bar and Twin Oaks are each and every one heavily frequented purveyors of Italian cuisine. Italian-influenced bakeries are also popular in the region, including Tomaro's, Abruzzino's and the legendary Country Club Bakery in Fairmont. There's also a new spate of bakeries building on Italian heritage but with decidedly modern twists.

If you are going to have baked goods, chances are you want coffee. And in West Virginia, as in the rest of America, coffee has reached a whole new level of popularity and expectation. Good businesspeople respond to demographics and market trends, and those who call the Mountain State home are no different. That spirit has given rise to popular new landmarks like Black Dog Coffee (Inwood), the Tip-Top (Thomas), the Appalachian Coffee House (Princeton), Lost River Trading Post (Wardensville) and the super-fun Hot Cup in Logan.

There are, of course, dining landmarks at the other end of the spectrum, part and parcel of the resorts and hotels that have catered to the state's business and tourist clientele for decades, if not centuries. The Blennerhasset Hotel (Parkersburg), the Bavarian Inn (Shepherdstown), Oglebay (Wheeling) and the historic Greenbrier Resort (White Sulphur Springs) are prime examples of venerated institutions of the hospitality industry, with menus that reflect that legacy.

They may not have the scale of a hotel or resort, but West Virginia bed-and-breakfasts quietly contribute to the state's culinary story, and if you've had breakfast at one, you'll know that's no exaggeration.

International cuisine continues to make its presence felt in West Virginia, contributing greatly to the diversity that often surprises visitors and is a source of joy to locals. The list of cuisines available is long and growing. Restaurants offering up Mexican and Asian dishes are perhaps to be expected, but the possibilities do not end there. Greek, Lebanese, African, Middle Eastern, Indian, Irish, German and Swiss cafés, restaurants and pubs dot the landscape, offering up resistance to the generic menus of the chains.

As enticing as all these commercial culinary efforts are, the reality is that most of the culinary activity in the state occurs within the home, and within that majority, the myriad practices, ingredients and traditions are for the most part reflective of national trends. Sure, there are regions within the state where negative food choices dominate. Processed foods, unhealthy fats and too much sugar contribute to high obesity rates in the state. In areas of poverty, food practices and choices are nearly always detrimental to the health of residents. It is maddening to realize that in a place as biodiverse as Appalachia, one with not only tremendous natural resources but also a heritage of subsistence farming and foraging, there should be such a disconnect from one's food; but that is a sad reality. The USDA defines a food desert as "parts of the country vapid of fresh fruit, vegetables, and other healthful whole foods, usually found in impoverished areas. This is largely due to a lack of grocery stores, farmers' markets, and healthy food providers." The good news is that state government as well as nonprofits, church groups, universities and other organizations like Grow Ohio Valley recognize this problem and are tackling it head on.

There are, however, many West Virginians who do recognize the value of fresh, healthy food and are taking steps to ensure they get it. As we have seen, the farmers' markets are doing very well. But many people are taking an even more proactive stance and bringing back the family garden. Growing your own food not only ensures that you know where and how some of your food was grown, but it also contributes to a family or individual's financial well-being and, perhaps most important of all, represents physical activity with proven health benefits. When we work in our gardens, we aren't sitting in front of a television or a computer. We are getting vitamin D from the sun and fresh air and gaining the mental and emotional boosts that come with a sense of accomplishment.

Of course, the level of complexity to a home garden can vary greatly. For some people, flowerpots or buckets that are planted with basil and tomatoes and line an apartment balcony constitute their "garden." For others, a small plot in the corner of the backyard delivers fresh squash and even a few ears of corn. A lot of folks are experimenting with raised beds and square-foot gardening and other space-saving attempts in what is known as bio-intensive gardening—which, among other things, attempts to maximize yield through improved soil health. Permaculture—a garden and farming practice meant to create interdependent growing systems that can be sustainable and self-sufficient—is gaining traction among a number of folks around the state. Home and garden centers and the big home improvement chains have expanded their offerings to cater to an obvious desire among West Virginians to pursue vegetable gardening and its rewards.

There also is renewed interest in historical practices of food preparation. Backyard bread ovens, small-scale maple sap tapping and meat smokers are just a few of these practices that folks are rediscovering and enjoying. They may not always represent the most cost-effective methods, but perhaps not every benefit they offer can be measured in dollars and cents. Whatever the rationale, a lot of West Virginians are at least partially reclaiming their culinary heritage.

As our story comes to a close, for now, consider this: for all these innovations and modernizing trends, for all the distractions of the modern world and the media and Internet and everything else that fights to capture our attention, there are some things that will continue on in West Virginia, as they have for centuries. In late March and early April, folks will scramble across forested hillsides in search of ramps and morels, and there will be ramp suppers and even people selling ramps out of cars alongside roads. In the summertime, someone will emerge from floating the Trough section of the South Branch and fry up some of the bass and bluegill they have caught, perhaps joined by a neighbor who has fried up the legs of bullfrogs they have gigged from a farm pond. Kids will miss school to go deer hunting in the fall, and venison sandwiches will still be served up at hunting camps. There will be chow chow canned in October, maple trees tapped in late winter and apple butter cooked up in pots and apples pressed for cider through the fall. Pita piatta (pitta m'pigliata) and pizzelles will be baked for the holidays, as will bread in backyard woodfired ovens all year round. Bacon will be cured, and beef jerky will be smoked. Free-range pigs will root through woodlots for acorns and, with any luck, returning American chestnuts, and moonshine, though no longer as exciting legally, will still be passed around campfires in mason jars. These things in no way are meant to represent the habits or interests or traditions of every single West Virginian. But they do represent much of the best the state has to offer— and not only in a culinary sense.

❖ ❖ ❖

Wanda's Salad Dressing

1 cup sugar
2 teaspoons flour
¼ cup white vinegar
Pinch of salt
¼ cup water

2 eggs, beaten
2 teaspoons prepared mustard
3 teaspoons celery seed
3 tablespoons mayo or salad dressing

In a bowl, add the sugar, flour, vinegar, salt and water. Add the eggs. Add to a nonreactive pan and cook over medium heat until thick, stirring constantly. Take off heat, then add the prepared mustard, celery seeds and salad dressing. Cover and let cool. Dress fresh greens.

❖ ❖ ❖

Chow Chow

1 head cabbage, cored and chopped
3 onions
3 green peppers
3 red peppers
3 green tomatoes
3 tablespoons salt
1 tablespoon ground mustard
¼ tablespoon turmeric
¼ tablespoon ginger
1 tablespoon mustard seed
¾ tablespoon celery seed
¼ tablespoon mixed whole spice
1 ¼ cups sugar
1 quart vinegar

Core the cabbage and then chop the cabbage, onions, peppers and tomatoes and mix together with salt. Let stand overnight. Drain. Tie mixed spices in a bag, add sugar and vinegar and add to the vegetable mixture. Simmer for 20 minutes. Remove spice bag. Pack into clean hot jars, leaving ¼ inch head space. Wipe the rims with a clean cloth and gently tighten lids. Place in the canner and cover with water. Bring water to a rapid boil and then process for another 10 minutes.

❖ ❖ ❖

Grandma Brookover's Pepper Rings

2 pounds Hungarian wax peppers
4 cups white vinegar
½ cup oil
2½ cups sugar
1 clove garlic
½ teaspoon salt

Clean peppers, take out seeds and cut into rings. Bring vinegar, oil and sugar to a boil. In a clean canning jar, add the pepper rings, 1 clove of garlic and ½ teaspoon of salt. Pour boiling liquid over the peppers until it covers them. Wipe the rims with a clean cloth and screw on lids. Cold pack in a hot water bath and process for 10 minutes. Great on sandwiches, hot dogs, pepperoni rolls or served with meat or antipasti platters.

❖ ❖ ❖

Blackberry Jelly

5 cups blackberries
2 cups sugar
Zest of one lemon

Combine the mashed berries and sugar, cover and let macerate in the refrigerator for 2 to 24 hours. In a non-reactive pan, bring to a boil and let the jam bubble, stirring regularly, until it reduces. Using a candy thermometer, monitor the cooking jam's temperature. When it reaches 220 degrees, remove it from the heat. Ladle into prepared jars, wipe rims, apply lids and rings and process in a boiling water canner for 15 minutes, if desired. This jam will keep for a couple of weeks in the fridge without processing.

❖ ❖ ❖

Apple Pie

The crust can also be made in a food processor.

For the crust:
2½ cups flour
1 teaspoon salt
½ cup shortening
5 tablespoons ice-cold water
For the filling:
1 cup sugar
1 tablespoon butter
1 tablespoon flour
5 large tart apples, sliced thin
Zest and juice of one lemon
1 teaspoon cinnamon
½ teaspoon nutmeg
½ teaspoon salt

Sift the flour and salt together. Cut in the shortening until mixture is coarse and granulated and looks like peas. Add the ice-cold water a little at a time and toss with a fork until moistened. Divide dough into 2 equal balls. Wrap in plastic wrap and chill for 30 minutes. Flatten out on a lightly floured surface. Roll out from center to edge until ⅛ inch thick.

Make the sugar mixture by combining 1 cup of sugar, 1 tablespoon of butter and 1 tablespoon flour. Put apples in a bowl, add lemon juice and zest and sprinkle generously with the sugar, spice mixture and salt. Fill pie crust with mixture and dot with butter. Cover top of pie with strips of pie pastry. If making a double crust, top with other pie dough then cut a few slits in the top so the steam escapes. Bake in a preheated 425-degree oven for 30 to 40 minutes.

❖ ❖ ❖

Blackberry Cake

3 cups blackberries
1 cup flour
1 cup sugar
2 teaspoons baking powder
1 teaspoon vanilla
2 eggs
½ cup shortening

In a mixing bowl, mash the berries with a fork. Add remaining ingredients except the shortening and beat well with a fork. Melt shortening and pour into the blackberry mixture. Mix well with a fork again. In a greased 9x13 pan, pour mixture and bake at 350 degrees for 30 to 45 minutes.

❖ ❖ ❖

Black Walnut Cake

1 cup ground coconut
¼ cup black walnuts, ground
¼ cup black walnuts, chopped
2 cups enriched flour, sifted
1 teaspoon baking soda
½ teaspoon cream of tartar
1 teaspoon salt
1 ½ cups sugar
½ cup Crisco
2 unbeaten eggs
½ teaspoon vanilla
½ teaspoon walnut flavor
1 cup buttermilk
½ cup strong black hot coffee

Add the coconut and walnuts together. Set aside. Sift together the flour, baking soda, cream of tartar and salt. Cream the sugar and

Crisco together. Slowly add the eggs and flavorings to the creamed mixture. Add the dry ingredients to the creamed ingredients a little at a time, alternating with a little buttermilk. Cream together on slow. Add the coffee and all but 3 tablespoons of the coconut-nut mixture. Fold in thoroughly. Grease two 8-inch greased and floured pans, then add cake batter. Bake at 375 degrees for 30 to 40 minutes. Cool before frosting.

❖ ❖ ❖

Coffee Frosting

4 cups sifted confectioners' sugar
4 tablespoons Crisco
½ teaspoon walnut flavor
½ teaspoon vanilla
⅛ teaspoon salt
2 tablespoons melted butter
3 tablespoons hot coffee

Combine sugar and Crisco. Add flavorings and salt. Add melted butter and coffee and beat until it is spreadable. Spread on cake and top with remaining coconut-nut mixture.

❖ ❖ ❖

Apple Butter

5 pounds apples (mix of golden delicious, Fuji, Rambo and Granny Smith)
3 cups water
½ cup apple cider vinegar
1 cup sugar
1 cup hard cider
2 cups honey
2 teaspoons cinnamon

1 teaspoon ground cloves
1 teaspoon ground allspice
1 teaspoon nutmeg
1 teaspoon ginger
A pinch of salt

Wash the apples in cool water. Slice apples into quarters or smaller pieces if using very large apples. Add the apples, water and vinegar to a crock pot, place on medium-high heat and cook overnight or 8 hours. Use a spoon to remove apples from liquid, and place apples in a food mill or sieve. Force the pulp through the sieve and place in a separate bowl below. Add the sugar, hard cider, honey, spices and salt to the apple puree. Stir well to incorporate all flavors. Place sauce pot over very low heat and let simmer for about 6 hours, stirring as needed to keep from burning. Mixture will thicken over time and splatter if not watched carefully.

When done, ladle into hot jars, leaving ¼ inch headspace. Remove air bubbles, clean rim, apply lid, apply band and tighten finger tight. Process 10 minutes using the water bath method.

❖ ❖ ❖

Pawpaw Bread

1 cup melted butter
2 cups sugar
4 eggs
1 teaspoon vanilla
2 cups pawpaw pulp
1 tablespoon lemon juice
2 teaspoons baking powder
½ teaspoon salt
4 cups flour, sifted
3 cups walnuts, chopped

Beat butter, sugar, eggs and vanilla. Add and beat in pawpaw pulp and lemon juice. Sift baking powder, salt and flour together and stir into batter. Stir in nuts and place evenly in the two oiled loaf pans. Bake in a preheated 375-degree oven for 1 hour and 15 minutes or until done.

❖ ❖ ❖

Persimmon Upside-Down Cake

¼ cup butter
2 cups brown sugar
1 egg
2 cups flour
½ teaspoon salt
2 teaspoons baking powder
1 cup persimmon pulp
½ cup nuts
1 cup water

Preheat oven to 350 degrees. Cream the butter and one cup of the brown sugar. Beat in the egg. Sift the flour, salt and baking powder and add alternately with the persimmon pulp to the creamed mixture. Stir in nuts. Heat remaining brown sugar with water until it boils. Cook for 1 minute. Pour into a loaf pan, then pour batter on top. Bake for 40 to 45 minutes.

SELECTED BIBLIOGRAPHY

Ambler, Charles H. *West Virginia: The Mountain State*. New York: Prentice-Hall, 1940.

Anderson, Kevin. "Sedor Fedukovich: A New American in Fayette County." *Goldenseal* 22, no. 3 (Fall 1996).

Anderson, Osbourn P. *A Voice from Harper's Ferry: A Narrative of Events at Harper's Ferry; with Incidents Prior and Subsequent to Its Capture by Captain Brown and His Men*. Ithaca, NY: Cornell University Library, 1861.

Brunvand, Jan Harold. *The Study of American Folklore*. New York: W.W. Norton & Company, 1998.

Conley, Phil, and William Thomas Doherty. *West Virginia History*. Charleston, WV: Charleston Education Foundation, 1974.

Core, Earl. L. *The Monongalia Story*. Parsons, WV: McClain Publishing Company, 1974.

Dayton, Ruth Woods. *Pioneers and Their Homes on Upper Kanawha*. Charleston: West Virginia Publishing Company, 1947.

Doddridge, Joseph. *Notes on the Settlement and Indian Wars of the Western Parts of Virginia and Pennsylvania*. N.p., 1824.

Dunnington, George. *History and Progress of the County, Marion*. Fairmont, WV: George Dunnington, 1880.

Eller, Ronald D. *Miners, Millhands and Mountaineers: Industrialization of the Appalachian South, 1880–1930*. Knoxville: University of Tennessee Press, 1982.

Fischer, David Hackett. *Albion's Seed: Four British Folkways in America*. New York: Oxford University Press, 1989.

Forsberg, Barbro, and Stefan Lindberg. *Edible Mushrooms: Safe to Pick, Good to Eat.* N.p.: Skyhorse Publishing, 2012.

Green, Janet W. *Women's Work in the Southern West Virginia Coal Camps.* Vol. 49 (1990): 37–54.

Gutheim, Frederick. *The Potomac.* Baltimore, MD: John Hopkins University Press, 1977.

Harmer, Harvey W. *Old Grist Mills of Harrison County.* N.p.: Charlestown Printing Company, 1940.

Harmer, Harvey, and Heisel Fox. *History of Worthington and Surrounding Communities.* Parsons, WV: McClain Publishing Company, 1968.

Harshbarger, Dwight. *Witness at Hawks Nest.* Huntington, WV: Mid-Atlantic Highlands, 2012

Kavasch, E. Barrie. *Native Harvests: American Indian Wild Foods and Recipes.* Mineola, NY: Dover Publications, 2005.

Lanning, Michael Lee. *The American Revolution 100: The People, Battles and Events of the American Revolution.* N.p.: Source Books, Inc., 2009.

Lewis, Virgil A. *History and Government of West Virginia.* Woodstock, GA: American Book Company, 1912.

Leyburn, James G. *The Scotch-Irish: A Social History.* Chapel Hill: University North Carolina Press, 1962.

Lough, Glenn. *Now and Long Ago.* Parsons, WV: McClain Publishing Company, 1969.

Marion County Historical Society. *A History of Marion County.* Fairmont, WV, 1985.

Maxwell, Hu. *The History of Barbour County, West Virginia.* Parsons, WV: McClain Publishing Company, 1899.

Morton, Oren F. *A History of Pendleton County, West Virginia.* Baltimore, MD: Regional Publishing Company, 1980.

Newman, Dora Lee. *Marion County in the Making.* Fairmont, WV: Francis Pierpont, 1917.

Price, William T. *Historical Sketches of Pocahontas County, West Virginia.* Marlinton, WV: Price Brothers, 1901.

Rakes, Paul H. "Casualties on the Homefront: Scotts Run Mining Disasters During World War II." *West Virginia History* 53 (1994): 95–118.

Rice, Otis. *West Virginia.* Lexington: University Press of Kentucky, 1985.

Ross, Phil. "The Scotts Run Coalfield from the Great War to the Great Depression: A Study in Overdevelopment." *West Virginia History* 53 (1994): 21–42.

Shifflett, Crandell A. *Coal Towns: Life, Work and Culture in Company Towns of Southern Appalachia, 1880–1960*. Knoxville: University of Tennessee Press, 1991.

Smith, Merrill D. *History of American Cooking*. Santa Barbara, CA: ABC-CLIO, 2013.

Smucker, Anna Egan. *A History of West Virginia*. N.p.: West Virginia Humanities Council, 1997.

Steelhammer, Rick. *It Happened in West Virginia*. N.p.: Morris Book Publishing, LLC, 2013.

Sullivan, Ken. *The West Virginia Encyclopedia*. N.p.: West Virginia Humanities Council, 2016.

Sutton, John Davison. *History of Braxton County and Central West Virginia*. N.p.: McClain Printing Company, 1997.

Thomas, Jerry Bruce: *An Appalachian New Deal: West Virginia in the Great Depression*. Lexington: University Press of Kentucky, 1998.

Turman, Jinny. "West Virginia History Lecture." West Virginia University, 2015.

Watson, James Otis, and the J.O. Watson Class of Fairmont High School. *Marion County in the Making*. Fairmont, WV, 1917.

Williams, John Alexander. *West Virginia: A History*. New York: Norton, 1984.

INDEX

ABOUT THE AUTHOR

Shannon Colaianni Tinnell is an author, historian and lover of Appalachian foods and foodways. Armed with a master's in public history from West Virginia University, Tinnell has written extensively on West Virginia history for publications like *Goldenseal* and on food and cooking for books and magazines. She contributed the cookbook section to the Eisner Award–nominated graphic novel *Feast of the Seven Fishes* and created and styled the on-screen food for the movie adaptation of the book. She resides with her husband, two children and one very spoiled dog.

Visit us at
www.historypress.com